Contents

A Pocket Book on

A natural food and a versatile ingredient

Octopus Books

A Pocket Book on

Cheese

A natural food and a versatile ingredient

Shirley Gill

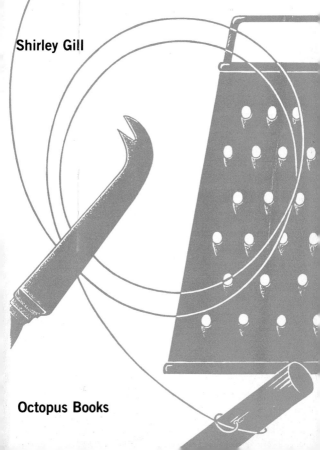

Octopus Books

Contents

First published 1985 by
Octopus Books Limited
59 Grosvenor Street
London W1

© 1985 Octopus Books Limited

ISBN 0 7064 2312 7

Produced by Mandarin Publishers Ltd
22a Westlands Road, Quarry Bay,
Hong Kong

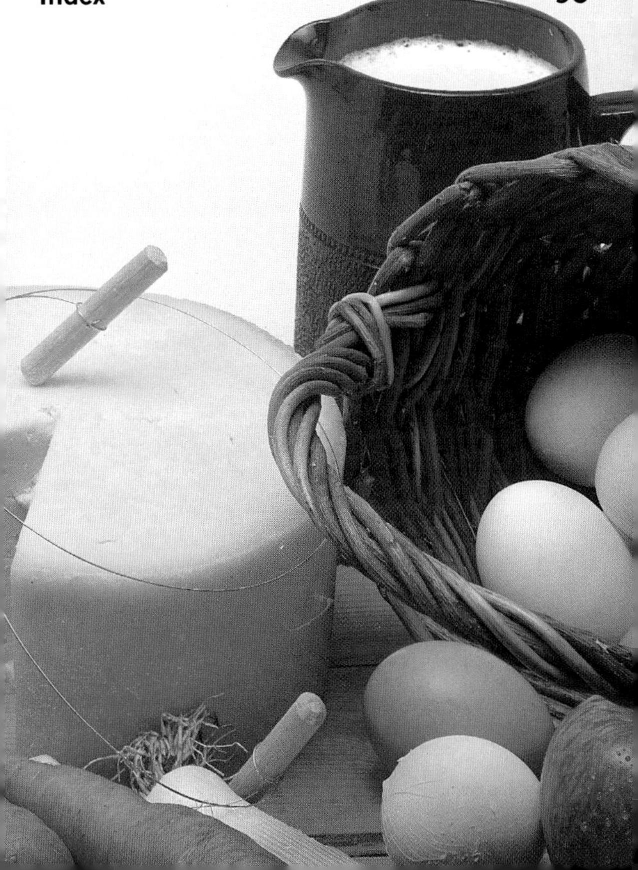

Introduction

Cheese is a simple food – a concentrated form of milk – yet the variations are seemingly endless. Every cheese has its own characteristic shape, size, colour and crust, producing a vast and exotic range of flavours, aromas and textures.

Cheeses owe their individual characteristics to a number of factors – quality and source of milk, manufacturing process, climate, and vegetation. Because of this, some cheeses cannot be reproduced outside their place of origin.

Whether served as a starter, main course, savoury, dessert, or snack, cheese is extremely versatile and highly nutritious. It is an excellent source of protein and calcium and provides appreciable amounts of vitamins A and D. It greatly enhances the flavour of many other foods and can be used to create a vast range of tasty and appetizing dishes. Yet it is also one of the very few foods that stand most successfully on their own.

This book gives information on buying, storing, serving and cooking cheese. There are useful tips on how to hold a successful cheese and wine party, plus a guide to the most notable cheeses. Some of the recipes in the book are traditional favourites, but there are many more unusual ones which demonstrate the versatility of cheese and offer inventive ideas for enjoying cheese to the full.

HISTORY

The origins of cheesemaking are intriguing. According to legend, it all began when an Asian nomad called Kanana crossed the desert with fresh milk in a pouch made from an animal's stomach. All day it hung from his saddle and by nightfall, the milk had coagulated due to the rennet in the lining of the animal's stomach. It was possibly the combination of heat and the movement of his mount that caused the separation of the curds and whey. Whether this *was* the beginning of cheesemaking will always remain a mystery. It is no longer necessary to trek across a desert to make cheese, but the principles remain the same – to solidify the milk by means of curdling and draining before a period of ripening. The final character of any one cheese is, however, dictated by the variations at each stage of production.

CHEESEMAKING

Separation

The first stage is always the separation of the milk solids (curds) from the liquid (whey).

The milk used may be partly or fully skimmed or it may be enriched with the addition of cream. At this early stage any of the following may be added: a dye such as annatto to promote colour; mould spores such as penicillium roquefortii to promote veining, or an acid bacteria to encourage the formation of holes.

The milk is then heated. Pasteurized milk requires the addition of a 'starter' (a laboratory grown culture with a high concentration of lactic acid) which increases the acidity of the milk and begins to turn it sour. Often rennet is added, causing a reaction in the milk which causes it to separate. The choice of whether to start with an acid curd cheese or a renneted cheese influences the final flavour.

Cutting and draining

Once separation begins the curds can be cut and drained. The amount of separation, the time it takes, the size of the cut, the method used and the temperature will determine the moisture content and consequently the final texture and flavour.

During the next stage of production the individual differences between the cheeses begin to emerge. The salted curds are now transferred to a mould to complete drainage. They may be left to firm naturally, or may be lightly or heavily pressed. The degree of pressure and length of time both influence the type of cheese eventually produced. After pressing, the cheese may be soaked in brine, waxed, smoked or left to ripen naturally.

Ripening

This last stage is an important one and it is during this time that the special characteristics develop such as the blue veins in Stilton or the naturally white mould on Camembert. Certain factors are carefully controlled – temperature, humidity, the amount of draught, the treatment of the rind and how frequently the cheese is turned. The period of ripening varies from 4 weeks to 3 years.

Classification

There are numerous ways of classifying cheese, but there is no generally accepted method. They can be classified according to country of origin, the type of milk from which they are made, methods of processing, texture, flavour and so forth. However, it is possible to distinguish basic families.

Fresh cheeses

These are soft cheeses, which include cottage cheese, curd cheese (small curd cottage cheese) and cream cheese. They are made from naturally soured milk, whole or skimmed milk or cream. Fresh cheeses are uncooked and unripened. They are coagulated with rennet or lactic acid. Double (heavy) cream cheese, however, is made from rich unpasteurized cream which is usually allowed to solidify naturally. It is then hung in fine muslin (cheese-cloth) to drain. These cheeses are usually rich and creamy though generally, fresh cheeses tend to be mild and moist.

Ripened unpressed cheeses

This classification is the most diverse and includes cheeses with bloomy, unwashed rinds and those with orange-brown washed rinds. Brie and Camembert are the most famous of the former. The rennet-curd for these cheeses is never cut and the whey drains naturally. They are quick-ripened for a month, during which time they develop a growth of penicillium candidum mould, which forms the floury crust. Nowadays this mould spore is introduced artificially by spraying the cheese, which is frequently brushed to obtain the desired thickness. The rinds of these cheeses may be eaten.

Washed rind cheeses include Munster and Pont l'Eveque. The method of production is similar except that the curd is broken up and stirred. The period of ripening varies from 1 to 2 months, during which time they are regularly washed with water, brine, wine or beer. This prevents the growth of mould but promotes the growth of bacteria which give these cheeses their characteristic rinds. The rinds of these cheeses are soft and damp and rather smelly. They are not usually eaten.

Making Cheddar cheese

Pressed uncooked cheeses

These are scalded cheeses which are lightly or heavily pressed. Cheshire and Caerphilly are lightly pressed cheeses, which means that some of the whey is still contained. This shortens the ripening period. Hard pressed cheeses differ only in that they undergo greater pressure for a longer period, which results in a much firmer texture (for example, Cheddar). Pressed uncooked cheeses are given rinds in a number of ways: Cheddar, for instance, is dipped in hot water to give a tough thin protective rind which is then salted and rubbed with fat and then bandaged with cloth.

Pressed cooked cheeses

This process – where the curds are cooked to produce a tougher and drier texture – is used for Emmental and Gruyère. They are then heavily pressed during which time they develop their characteristic 'holey' appearance.

Pasta Filata cheeses

The Italian translation for pasta filata is 'spun paste', a reference to the fact that the curds are immersed in hot water, kneaded and stretched to the desired consistency, then moulded to the required shape. Provolone and Mozzarella are in this category.

Whey cheeses

These are made from the liquid that separates from the curds when the milk and rennet are heated together. They are formed by the solidification of the albumen contained in the whey. Milk is sometimes added to the hot whey to make a richer cheese. Ricotta is a prime example of a fresh whey cheese.

Blue cheeses

Blue cheeses are created by the addition of special bacteria to the curds to create the distinctive blue or greenish-blue veining. Originally, these blue veins developed naturally from moulds in the atmosphere. Nowadays the curds are innoculated with penicillium roquefortii before being cut, drained and packed in moulds. They are turned over and drained frequently until the recognizable cheeses are formed, though at this stage they are white and tasteless. The next stage is to prick the cheeses all over with steel needles to create air passages which enable the mould to travel through the cheeses. The cheeses are then ripened in controlled conditions for weeks or months, depending on the cheese. During this time they are regularly turned and checked until the mould is fully developed. The classic blues are Gorgonzola, Roquefort and Stilton. Other blue cheeses include Bleu d'Auvergne, Danablu and Pipo Crem' to name but a few.

Goats' milk and sheep's milk cheeses

These are most widely produced in France, Greece, central Europe, Italy and the Middle East. Goats' milk is increasingly being mixed with cows' milk because goats' lactation periods are short and therefore seasonal. Most goats' milk cheeses are ripened for only a short period, though a few have washed rinds and are sold highly ripened. Generally, they are moist and smooth with a strong, full flavour.

Sheep's milk cheeses are always sharper in flavour than cows' milk cheeses and range from semi-soft to very hard in texture. They are not generally heavily pressed. Greek Feta, for example, has lightly pressed curds. Feta cheese is actually soaked in salted whey and left to ripen in it for a short time — which is why it is often salty.

Processed cheeses
These are made by blending natural cheese with emulsi-
fiers, additives and flavourings. Their consistency can
range from firm to soft and spreadable and their flavour
usually lacks character. Most processed cheeses are
Cheddar based or made from surplus supplies of Emmental or Gruyère.

Nutritional value

Cheese has a high nutritional value which is not surprising
when you consider that it takes 600 ml/1 pint (2½ cups) of
milk just to produce 50 g (2 oz) of cheese. As it is a
concentrated form of milk it benefits from all the milk
nutrients. Most of the protein, fat and vitamin A remain in
the curd after it has been separated while a large part of the
carbohydrate (lactose) and B vitamins are lost in the whey.

Cheese can regularly be included in the diet during all
stages of life – babies as young as nine months old can
easily assimilate grated mild cheese. It is an ideal snack to
give to children who do not like milk. Cheese provides a
good source of protein to adolescents, pregnant and nurs-
ing mothers. Some of the light cheeses such as Caerphilly
are invaluable in invalid diets where easily digested foods
are required.

Composition
The nutritional value of cheese varies according to the milk
from which it was made and its method of production, but
it can be said that soft cheeses with a high moisture
content have a lower percentage of nutrients than hard
cheese.

Protein Cheese is an excellent source of first class protein
in the form of caseinogen – weight for weight more than
raw meat. It is a must for vegetarians as a chief source of
protein.

Fat The subject of fat is a confusing one – the fat content of
cheese is expressed as a measure of the dry matter, not the
cheese as a whole. A high moisture cheese will have a
lower fat content than a low moisture cheese of the same

weight. For example, Camembert and Emmental both have the same fat content of 45 per cent but 125 g/4 oz (¼ lb) of Emmental will have a higher fat content than the same amount of Camembert because Emmental contains less moisture.

Cheeses made from whole milk have a higher fat content than those made from skimmed milk (such as cottage cheese); similarly those made from cream have a particularly high fat content.

Carbohydrate Almost all cheeses have a low sugar content except whey cheeses like Ricotta.

Minerals Cheese is one of the best sources of calcium and phosphorus. 50 g/2 oz of any hard cheese contains more calcium than the same amount of bread, 300 ml/½ pint (1¼ cups) of milk or 1 egg.

Vitamins The vitamin content varies according to the quality of the milk, and the changes that occur during ripening and storage. Cheese, especially that made from summer milk, is a rich source of vitamin A. It is also a good source of riboflavin, which is partly combined with the caseinogen and so remains in the curd when the milk separates. Vitamins A and D are both fat-soluble so the higher the fat content the greater the concentration of these vitamins in the cheese.

Fibre Cheese is not regarded as a source of fibre but when eaten with bread, especially wholewheat bread, it makes a well-balanced snack.

Cheese and slimming
Slimmers often deny themselves cheese on the basis that it contains too many calories. But cheese is such a nutritious food that it's a shame to exclude it from the diet.

Cut down on quantity and choose cheeses with low calorific value such as cottage cheese, skimmed milk soft cheese, Gouda, Edam, Ricotta, Mozzarella and Feta.

Cheesemakers now also produce a firm cheese which resembles Cheddar but has only half the fat, and just over half the calories of its look-alike.

Energy value of some popular cheeses (per 25 g/1 oz)

Type	Cal	Type	Cal
Appenzell	113	Emmental	113
Bel Paese	96	Feta	54
Boursin	116	Gorgonzola	112
Brie	88	Gouda	100
Caerphilly	120	Gruyère	132
Camembert	88	Lancashire	109
Cheddar	120	Mozzarella	87
Cheshire	110	Leicester	105
Cottage cheese	27	Parmesan	118
Cream cheese	125	Port Salut	94
Curd cheese	40	Ricotta	55
Danish Blue	103	Roquefort	88
Derby	110	Skimmed milk soft	
Dolcelatte	100	cheese	25
Double Gloucester	105	Stilton	131
Edam	88	Wensleydale	115

Cottage cheese is ideal for slimmers

Buying cheese

Try always to buy cheeses from a reputable shop, preferably a specialist store with a good turnover. An invitation to taste before you buy is a sign of a good cheese counter and means you can avoid buying anything that does not suit your palate. The flavour of freshly cut cheese tends to be better than that of pre-wrapped pieces.

Once a cheese has matured it does not improve with keeping, especially when cut, so buy day to day rather than stocking up on supplies.

Avoid any cheeses that look dry, are too hard, too crumbly or show signs of sweating, oiliness or mould where no mould should be. Beware, too, sourness and excessive pungency.

Prepacked cheeses should be checked for date of sale and the packaging should not look smeared or puffed up. Always read the instructions on the wrapping regarding opening, storing and serving – these should be strictly observed.

Examine all labels as many cheeses are now subject to legal protection – for example, authentic Parmigiano-Reggiano (Parmesan) cheeses have the name stencilled on the rind.

Storing cheese

Ideally one should store cheese as little as possible and certainly in quantities that can be consumed quickly. Keep all cheeses in a cool place such as the larder or in the refrigerator wrapped in plastic wrap, foil or in an airtight container. Some cheeses, such as Parmigiano-Reggiano (Parmesan), are best wrapped in a damp cloth. Always wrap them individually to avoid mingling of flavours. Remember that cheeses need to be taken out of the refrigerator and brought back to room temperature at least an hour before serving.

Freezing cheese

As a rule, the higher the fat content, the better the cheese will freeze. The recommended minimum fat content for

cheeses to be frozen is 45 per cent. When freezing cheeses:
- Ensure the cheeses are in prime condition.
- Wrap all cheese in special freezer coverings.
- When thawing, return to the refrigerator to allow the full flavour to develop.
- Always thaw frozen cheese thoroughly before use whether it is for cooking or for eating.
- Never freeze blue cheese – the texture will be spoilt and its odour will be transmitted to other foods. It also deteriorates quickly once it has thawed.
- It is handy to have bags of grated cheese in the freezer for emergencies, otherwise store in 250 g/8 oz (½ lb) quantities.

Serving cheese

To enjoy cheese at its best, most should be served at room temperature. Remove from the refrigerator about 30 to 60 minutes before serving. Cream cheeses are the exception and are usually served lightly chilled. Avoid letting the cheese become too warm as this can lead to sweating and changes in flavour. Never unwrap cheese until just before serving to prevent drying out and exchanges of aromas.

The question often arises as to when the cheese course should be served. In England we tend to serve it after the dessert, whereas in France it follows the salad and is served before the dessert. In Greece, it is often served as a side dish with the main meal.

Cheese is also served at different times of the day. In Germany and Holland, for instance, they eat it for breakfast; in Portugal and Spain they often have it as an appetizer and in England the 'Ploughman's lunch' of cheese, bread, ale and pickle is a classic favourite.

Display cheeses attractively on a cheeseboard or platter with a garnish of parsley, watercress, celery sticks (stalks) or a small bunch of grapes.

Choose the cheese for the occasion – for lunch a choice of 2 hard cheeses, one strong and one mild is adequate. For a formal dinner party offer a wider selection, including some of the more unusual varieties, or go to the other extreme and serve a single cheese such as Stilton.

Where possible offer a selection of fruit and interesting bread and biscuits (crackers); like water biscuits, Bath Olivers, bran or semi-sweet biscuits. The connoisseurs, however, recommend that you serve cheese with fruit alone.

As presentation is so important, remember to remove all boxes, wrappings and inedible rinds before serving and bear in mind that how they are served can greatly influence the enjoyment of many cheeses. Some are sliced, others spread while some are best spooned.

Cooking with cheese

Whatever cheese you are using, the basic principle is to melt the cheese over a low heat rather than cook it. Too high a temperature will cause the cheese to curdle. Too rapid heating will cause the cheese to become stringy. When grilling (broiling) place it under a moderate heat for just long enough to melt it, rather than under a fierce heat for a shorter time.

Cheese soufflé is one of the classic cheese dishes

The texture of a particular cheese is a clear indication of its best use in cooking — hard cheeses can be grated and are invaluable in soups, sauces and soufflés. Cheddar is good in quiches and bakes. Gruyère needs to be grated more coarsely but is a good melting cheese, especially in fondues. Lancashire and Leicester are generally the best for toasting. Cream cheeses blend well with eggs and are therefore ideal in savoury custards and baked cheesecakes. Cheeses such as Brie often need to be cut up and gently melted if they are to be combined with other ingredients. Some cheeses such as Mozzarella, need only be thinly sliced. Blue cheeses can be cooked, but when they are in peak condition they are best enjoyed as they are. They do, however, add a delightful tang to fondues, pastries, breads, stuffings, vegetable dishes and flans.

Cheese and wine parties

A cheese and wine party is an excellent way of entertaining friends, regardless of the numbers involved. Like any party, much of the success depends upon plenty of advance planning and attention to detail. But whatever the scale or degree of sophistication, when you are planning a cheese and wine party, there are certain points to consider.

● Buy as interesting an assortment of cheeses as you can find and afford, selecting cheeses to complement and contrast with each other as regards colour, texture and flavour.

● Select wines with care. They should complement the cheese (see page 17).

● Check your supply of glasses, cheeseboards, breadbaskets, butter dishes, napkins, cutlery and crockery, and arrange to hire, if necessary.

● Make shopping lists — the first for items that can be bought in advance and the second for last-minute things such as fresh cheeses, fruit, vegetables and bread.

Cheeses

Offer a wide selection of cheeses including hard, soft, strong, mild, and blue-veined. Obvious choices include a whole Brie, Cheddar or Stilton, but try some of the less well known cheeses like Bleu de Bresse, Boursault, Chevres, Pipo Crem', Torta San Gaudenzio, for a change. Ideally, you should have at least one creamy white, one blue and a hard cheese for your guests to sample.

Quantities

Allow 75-125 g/3-4 oz per person. If you offer a selection of canapes and dips as well, the quantity can be reduced. Make sure you have plenty of butter dishes on the table allowing 15 g/½ oz (1 tablespoon) per person or approximately 250 g/8 oz (1 cup) for every 15 to 20 people. Allow 1 French loaf between 3 or 4 people plus 3 or 4 biscuits. It is always better to have a little left over than not to have enough.

Presentation

Presentation is all important with party food. Arrange the cheeses either on traditional plain wooden boards, marble slabs, or a selection of contrasting plates. You can improvize with a bread board or table mat. A garnish of a few sticks (stalks) of celery, parsley, or a small bunch of black or white grapes enhances the cheeseboard. But if you are serving a selection of more unusual cheeses they are best left to speak for themselves. Ensure the cheese goes to the table looking appetizing and in prime condition. The cheeses are best arranged separately, to keep the flavours apart, and a cheese knife should be placed alongside each. Never place them on paper or linen napkins; in the heat of the room the cheese may melt and stick to them. Present the cheeses either by country of origin, type, or in a tasting order — from mildest to strongest.

Accompaniments

A few choice accompaniments can be served with the cheese to complement rather than mask the flavours and also to enhance the display. Serve a selection of breads, rolls and crispbreads and an assortment of biscuits (crackers). Heat a few French bread loaves in the oven. Serve lots of fresh celery. Cucumber sticks, baby carrots and radishes are easier to cope with than bowls of salads. They also provide a refreshing contrast to some of the richer cheeses. Remember the food should not be messy or fiddly and must be easy to eat. Cheese straws (page 89) are always popular, so are dips. The cocktail cheesecake (page 91) is delicious and makes a welcome change. For hot dishes try Camembert Beignets (page 92) or Auvergne Triangle's (page 88). Try to select items which can be prepared in advance and avoid last minute attention.

Always provide bowls of fruit – apples, black and white grapes, pineapples, pears and oranges all go particularly well with cheese. Some fruits form favoured combinations such as apples and Wensleydale or pears and Gorgonzola. Finally, round the evening off with fresh coffee.

Wines
The combination of wine and cheese is a classic one, a 'bon mariage' as the French would say. Yet it isn't so simple – there are so many varieties of cheese and wine that the combinations are endless.

Choose wines to suit the cheeses being served – strong pungent cheeses go well with young, full-bodied red wines or sweet whites. Soft cheeses and those of milder flavour require more subtle wines. If, however, you are having a large party it is best to serve one type of red and one white.

Cheese and wine combinations
Appenzell – *Beaujolais*
Bel Paese – *Valpolicella, Chianti*
Bleu d'Auvergne – *Châteauneuf-du-Pape*
Bleu de Bresse – *Saint-Émilion*
Boursin – *dry white wines from the Loire Valley, Mâcon*
Brie – *Sancerre, Bordeaux reds, Frascati*
Caerphilly – *Moselle, Soave, Vinho Verde*
Camembert – *Bordeaux reds, white Burgundy*
Cheddar – *Châteauneuf-du-Pape, Chianti Classico, Barolo*
Cheshire – *Beaujolais, Bull's Blood*
Chèvres – *Burgundy, Cabernet Sauvignon*
Danablu – *Rhône reds, Rioja*
Derby – *Bergerac, Côtes du Roussillon*
Double Gloucester – *Médoc, Barbaresco*
Edam – *light fruity reds or whites*
Emmental – *Niersteiner, fruity reds or whites*
Feta – *Retsina*
Gorgonzola – *Barolo*

Gouda – *Côtes du Rhône*
Gruyère – *Pinot Noir, Neuchâtel*
Havarti – *dry light whites*
Lancashire – *Alsace white*
Leicester – *Valpolicella, Mâcon Rouge*
Limburger – *full bodied reds, Châteauneuf-du-Pape*
Mozzarella – *Chianti*
Münster – *Pinot Noir, Gewürztraminer*
Pont l'Eveque – *Saint-Émilion, Côtes du Roussillon*
Port Salut – *Beaujolais, Côtes du Rhône*
Provolone – *Chianti, Valpolicella*
Parmesan – *Lambrusco, Chianti*
Reblochon – *Muscadet, Chablis, Beaujolais*
Roquefort – *Sauternes*
Samsoe – *light reds and whites*
Stilton – *Barsac, Barola, Rioja, Port*
Teleggio – *Chianti, Valpolicella*
Tilsit – *light fruity reds*
Wensleydale – *Rosé d'Anjou, Laski Riesling*

Beer and cider are also natural accompaniments to many cheeses, especially those flavoured with added chives, pickle, wine and onions. For those that do not drink wine offer mineral water or fruit juices.

Chill white wine for at least an hour before serving and keep it cool during the party either in the fridge or in wine buckets with extra ice. Red wine is best served at room temperature, so open at least half the bottles ahead of time to let the flavour develop.

Quantities

On average allow half a bottle per person, but do keep a few extra bottles in reserve. Check whether it makes financial sense to buy wine by the case, boxes of wine or large bottles. When buying wines, bear in mind that some merchants will supply on a sale or return basis. Make sure that you try the wines in advance in case they do not suit the food that has been prepared. Take advice from your wine merchant, he is the expert! When choosing glasses, remember the larger the glass the more people tend to drink; 175 ml/6 fl oz (¾ cup) is a good size. The ideal glass should have a stem and a reasonably sized bowl.

Types of Cheese

British Cheeses

Blue Wensleydale
A close-textured blue veined cheese which has a much more robust flavour than the white version. It is considered a delicacy and is not easy to find, perhaps because it is now only made by one dairy in the Dove Valley of Derbyshire.

Caboc
Scottish double (heavy) cream cheese which is rolled in oatmeal. It has a creamy but somewhat bland flavour.

Caerphilly
Originating in Wales, it now ranks as an English cheese because it is produced mainly in the commercial creameries of Somerset and Wiltshire. It is a white, moist and crumbly cheese which has a salty, sour buttermilk flavour.

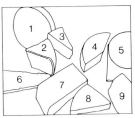

1 Leicester 2 Sherwood 3 Shropshire Blue 4 Stilton 5 Double Gloucester 6 Sage Derby 7 Cheddar 8 Lancashire 9 Windsor Red

Cheddar

The most famous of English cheeses, Cheddar has a waxy, close texture and colour which varies from pale straw to golden yellow. The flavour ranges from sweet and mild when young to rich and nutty when mature (sharp). Cheddar is the most imitated of cheeses and produced in many other countries such as New Zealand and Ireland. But the original English Cheddar is still the most popular, especially Farmhouse Cheddar, which varies slightly in flavour depending on which farm it comes from, but is always nutty, full-flavoured and strong. Cheddar has a close, buttery texture, which should not crumble or flake when cut.

Cheshire

Said to be the oldest of English cheeses, this was mentioned in the Domesday Book. It comes in 3 versions, white, red (stained with a natural vegetable dye from the seeds of the annatto tree), and blue. The white and red Cheshires are mild-flavoured, slightly salty and crumbly in texture. Blue Cheshire is considered a great delicacy. It is pale orange-gold in colour with striking blue veins running through it. It has a very creamy, strong flavour.

Cotswold

A modern creation — Double Gloucester flavoured with chopped chives and onion.

Cottage Cheese

A low-fat cheese made from the curds of skimmed milk, which have been washed and rinsed thoroughly. It has a mild flavour and granular texture.

Cream Cheese

Made from either single (light) or double (heavy) cream as the name suggests. It must have a fat content of at least 45 per cent. If it contains 65 per cent it is called Double Cream Cheese.

Curd Cheese

White with a smooth yet slightly granular texture. It has a mellow, slightly acid flavour. Available with low or medium fat content and a maximum moisture content of 70 per cent, curd cheese does not have a long shelf life and should be eaten as soon as possible after buying.

Derby

Derby has the distinction of being the first English cheese

to have been made in a creamery in 1870. Flaky and moist in texture, with a mild and delicate flavour. It is at its best at about 6 months, but unfortunately it is almost always sold far too young.

Double Gloucester

Bright orange, waxy cheese with a mature, creamy and delicate taste. Originally the cheese was exclusively made from the milk of the Gloucester cattle, a breed that is now almost extinct. Today, most Double Gloucester is creamery made, from a thinner milk than formerly, but it is still a rich cheese, especially if it is made from midsummer milk and matured for 9 months or more. Double Gloucester gets its name from its size, which is twice that of single Gloucester.

Dunlop

Mainly found in Scotland, it is a smooth, creamy white cheese. Its name originates from the village in Ayrshire where it was first made. Nowadays, Dunlop is entirely creamery made, although not in Dunlop itself.

Full Fat Soft Cheese

Has a rich creamy flavour and must contain at least 20 per cent milk fat and not more than 60 per cent water.

Lancashire

White cheese with a soft and crumbly texture, it has a mild flavour which develops a richness with maturity. It is the ultimate toasting cheese and was once known as 'Leigh Toaster' because of its suitability for Welsh Rarebit. A superior version is made from unpasteurized milk on 5 farms in the Preston area, otherwise it is all creamery made. Also available is Sage Lancashire which is Farm-house Lancashire flavoured with chopped sage.

Leicester

A hard-pressed granular cheese, which has a rich russet-red colour. It is moister than Cheddar and therefore has a shorter shelf life, reaching its peak at about 6 months old. Avoid cheese with white patches on the outer edges as these are signs of bitterness.

Lymeswold

A mild blue full fat soft cheese with a fresh creamy flavour and edible soft white rind.

Orkney

Small soft cheeses made from cows' milk, in the Orkneys. Available white, coloured and smoked; sometimes

matured in a barrel of oatmeal. Another island cheese from
Scotland is Islay which is very similar.

Sage Derby
Derby cheese flavoured with chopped sage leaves, it has a
distinctive green marbled effect.

Sherwood
Double Gloucester flavoured with sweet pickle.

Shropshire Blue
Dark orange cows' milk cheese with deep blue veins and a
strong piquant flavour.

Skimmed Milk Soft Cheese
This type of cheese must contain less than 2 per cent milk
fat and not more than 80 per cent water. It is soft and
smooth with a slightly acid taste.

Stilton
Blue Stilton is the 'King of Cheeses'. Made from cows' milk
and cream, it is a firm and creamy white cheese with a
distinctive blue veining. It has a naturally rough, crumbly
brown crust which is slightly wrinkled with white powdery
patches. The flavour ranges from mild when young to rich
and tangy when fully matured. Its origins are somewhat
obscure, but we do know that it takes its name from the
small village of Stilton in Huntingdonshire. Stilton is at its
best when fully ripe at 3 to 5 months. As the cheese ages
the mould spreads and the flavour deepens. When buying
a Stilton select one in which the veins are distributed
evenly throughout the paste and where there is a good
contrast between the paste and the blue veins. Traditionally Stilton is served with port.

Helpful Hint
When serving a whole Stilton, remove the top rind in a
single level slice. Then, moving down the cheese, cut
horizontal slices about 5 cm/2 inches thick, and cut these
into wedges to serve. After the meal replace the top rind as
a cover.

Wensleydale
The original Wensleydale was made from ewes' milk. It was
a soft, blue-veined cheese which was introduced into
England after the Norman Conquest. However, after the
Dissolution of the Monasteries in the 16th century,

Wensleydale began to be made from cows' milk by generations of farmers' wives. Production later moved to the small dairies. It is now usually sold before being fully ripened – at about a month old – as it is not a cheese that improves with age.

White Stilton
White and crumbly, White Stilton is made in the same way as Blue Stilton except it does not have the addition of penicillium roquefortii and so does not develop a mould. It has a much milder but slightly sour flavour.

Windsor Red
A deep pink, marbled cheese, made by flavouring Cheddar cheese with elderberry wine.

French Cheeses

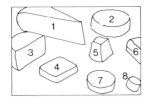

1 French Emmental (see p.29) 2 Saint Paulin 3 Roquefort 4 Pont l'Evèque 5 Pyramide de Valençay (see Chèvres) 6 Fondu aux Noix (see p.33) 7 Camembert 8 Rigotte de Condrieu

Bleu d'Auvergne
A very pale cheese with sharply defined blue veins. Rich, with a sharp salty flavour and a texture which is creamy

rather than crumbly. It originated in the 19th century as an imitation of Roquefort using cows' milk instead of sheep's milk. It is thought to be less delicate than Roquefort but similar in size and shape.

Bleu de Bresse

A soft and creamy dark blue-veined cheese, made from unskimmed cows' milk. Avoid over-ripe Bleu de Bresse as it turns grey and acquires a strong and unpleasant flavour.

Boursault

Small, triple-cream cheese, made from pasteurized milk. Very rich and creamy with a soft rind tinged with pink. Avoid those with red surfaces. A herb flavoured variety is also available.

Boursin

Brand name of a soft cream cheese made from enriched cows' milk. It has a rich and creamy flavour and is available flavoured with garlic, herbs or crushed peppercorns. Best eaten fresh.

Brie

One of the most famous French cheeses. Made from cows' milk, it is a soft, pale cheese with a delicate creamy flavour. It has a white floury crust instead of the more usual hard rind. There are numerous variations of Brie but among the most well known are: Brie Fermier, made in the Île de France from unpasteurized milk, and considered by some to be the best; Brie Laitier, made from pasteurized milk and factory produced. There are also variations such as herb, mushroom and pepper flavoured Brie. Brie is at its best when plump and smooth but not runny. It should smell fresh and pleasantly mouldy. Avoid any that smell of ammonia as this means the cheese is overripe.

Helpful Hint

Avoid Brie if it has a chalky band running through it – the outside will become overripe and taste of ammonia before the centre has time to mature.

Camembert

Made originally in Normandy, but now in other parts of France, Camembert is now mostly factory produced from pasteurized milk. Prepared in small rounds, it is a creamy, pale yellow cheese with a soft, smooth rind. When ripe,

Camembert should be soft and just bulge from the crust but not run.

Caprice des Dieux
Oval, double (heavy) cream cheese, which has a rich, mild and creamy flavour.

Chaumes
Made in the Dordogne, Chaumes has a deep orange coloured rind and rich creamy paste. It is made from pasteurized milk, and has a full, nutty flavour.

Chèvre
The generic name for goats' milk cheeses. There are many varieties which are made all over France. Cheese labelled 'Pur Chèvre' must by law be made entirely of goats' milk, others may be mixed with cows' milk and are known as 'mi-Chèvre'. Textures vary from soft, moist and creamy to dry and hard as they mature. They are small and moulded into many shapes – small discs, logs, cones, pyramids and cylinders. Chèvres always have a strong flavour – fresh and tart. Examples include Valençay, Chèvrotin and Saint Maure.

Coeurmandie
Heart shaped soft cheese similar in flavour and texture to Brie.

Demi-Sel
A small square shaped fresh cream cheese, made mainly in Normandy.

Excelsior
A double cream cheese from Normandy, mild and delicate in flavour with a very smooth texture.

Explorateur
A rich cream cheese with a mild flavour. Explorateur has a light coating of white rind and soft ivory paste.

Fontainebleau
A factory made, unsalted fresh cream cheese enriched with whipped cream.

Fromage Blanc
A low fat fresh rennet-curd cheese, which has a light, clean taste.

Munster
Said to be one of the oldest cheeses, dating back to the Middle Ages, Munster originated in a monastery in Alsace where it was first made by Irish Benedictine monks. It

takes its name from the Latin word for monastery. A round flat cheese made from cows' milk, it has a smooth, soft consistency. Munster Fermier (Farmhouse type) has a cloudy rind while the creamy version (Munster Laitier) has an orange-red rind. It is sometimes flavoured with cumin or aniseed.

Neufchâtel

Famous cheese from Normandy, often heart-shaped. Neufchâtel has a slightly salty flavour and is best eaten when fresh.

Petit Suisse

A soft, fresh cheese enriched with cream. Very mild in flavour, with a moist consistency. Petit Suisse is sold in small cylindrical shapes, individually wrapped.

Pipo Crem'

Creamy blue veined cheese with a rich, salty flavour.

Pont l'Evêque

Square shaped cheese with a smooth, golden yellow rind and pale yellow paste. A particularly strong smelling cheese with a rich fruity tang.

Port Salut

Port Salut was first made by the monks at the Abbey of Port du Salut in the early 1800s. Its orange rind encloses a smooth yellow interior, which is very mild in flavour when young but gets progressively stronger as it matures.

Reblochon

Reblochon comes from the Savoie region, it is a soft cheese with a mild, creamy and fruity flavour.

Rigotte

Tiny, round cows' or cows' and goats' milk cheeses. The best known are Rigotte de Condrieu and Rigotte des Alpes.

Roquefort

The most famous of the French blue-veined cheeses, Roquefort is unique as the only renowned blue cheese made with sheep's milk. A mould is added to the cheese curds to give the characteristic veining (more green than blue). They are left to age in the limestone caves of Columbou near Roquefort where the air currents provide ideal conditions for the development of the mould.

Roulé

A full fat soft cheese made with a special blend of garlic and fine herbs.

Saint Paulin
A factory made cheese similar to Port Salut. It has a bright orange rind and smooth, buttery yellow paste, with a mild, somewhat bland flavour.

Tartare
A garlic and herb flavoured soft cheese made in Périgard from pasteurized cows' milk.

Italian Cheeses

Bel Paese
Soft cheese with a creamy, slightly sweet taste.

Caciocavalla
Spun curd cheeses, with a smooth, yellowish rind.

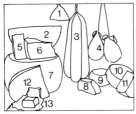

1 Mozzarella 2 Fontina 3 Provolone 4 Caciocavalla 5 Dolcelatte 6&7 Parmesan 8 Ricotta 9 Pecorino 10 Bel Paese 11 Gorgonzola 12 Italian Emmental (see p.29) 13 Robiola

Dolcelatte
This is a milder, creamier version of Gorgonzola (see below). It has a creamy moist texture, off-white in colour with blue-green veins running through it.

Fontina
Produced in the Alps near the borders of France and Switzerland, Fontina has a delicate nutty flavour. It has a light brown, slightly oiled rind and a straw coloured paste that has a few small round holes.

Gorgonzola
Probably the best known Italian cheese, named after the village of Gorgonzola near Milan. The cheese has a soft texture and is straw coloured with blue-green veining. Gorgonzola can be one of the most pungent and strong flavoured of the blues. It is at its best when firm and fairly dry.

Helpful Hint
Blue cheeses are best bought freshly cut from the whole cheese. The surface should be creamy and crumbly, white or yellowish with veining of an even colour. Avoid blue cheeses that show signs of sweating or have a dull bloom. Both these signs show that the cheese has not been cut for some time, a sure indication of a poor turnover.

Mascarpone, Mascherpone
A delicious soft cheese originally produced in Lombardy. Mascarpone is so creamy and mild that it is often served with fresh fruit or flavoured with powdered chocolate or coffee, or liqueurs.

Mozzarella
Traditionally made from water buffalos' milk, today those that are exported are made from cows' milk. The delicate flavour of Mozzarella means it should, ideally, be eaten as soon as possible after buying. A lightly smoked version is also available.

Parmesan (Parmigiano-Reggiano)
Dating back to about 1200 AD Parmesan is one of the world's most renowned hard-grating cheeses. It is made with milk from the provinces of Parma, Reggio Emilia, Modena, Bologna and part of Mantua and is only produced between 1st April and 11th November. Partly skimmed

unpasteurized cows' milk is used and it takes between 1 and 4 years to mature. The cheeses are sold at 4 stages – Giovane which is young Parmesan, Vecchio, Stravecchio and Stravecchione which are progressively older, harder and more flavoured. It is available by the piece or ready-grated and can be rather expensive.

Helpful Hint
Add grated Parmesan or Cheddar to rice dishes before serving for extra flavour.

Pecorino
There are several varieties of Pecorino cheese but all are made from sheep's milk and have a slightly sharp flavour.

Provolone
A smooth, creamy, dense cheese which is made from cows' milk coagulated either with calves' rennet (sweeter types), or kids' rennet (sharper types). It is delicate and mild when young and piquant when matured.

Ricotta
Fresh, white soft cheese with a fine granular consistency. It has a mild flavour verging on sweetness.

Robiola
A quick-ripening, soft cheese from northern Italy.

Taleggio
Creamy cheese which, when young, is mild and fruity. As it matures the flavour deepens. It has a white paste and pinkish-grey rind.

Torta San Gaudenzio
Made from alternate layers of Gorgonzola and Mascarpone.

German and Swiss Cheeses

Appenzell
A hard Swiss cheese, with a fruity flavour. During ripening it is steeped in wine, cider, herbs and spices.

Cambozola
A full-fat soft German cheese with an edible mould crust and blue-veined creamy paste. The flavour should be creamy and the blue veins give it a 'bite'.

Emmental
The name originates from the Emmen Valley near Bern

where it was first made. It is a dull, yellow cheese, with evenly distributed, small walnut-sized holes. It has a sweet, nutty flavour. One of the most popular European cheeses, the French and Italians make their own versions.

Gruyère
A hard Swiss cheese, similar to Emmental but with a much fuller, fruitier flavour. The holes are also smaller and the cheese a pale shade of yellow. It is made around Lake Gruyère from the milk of a breed of cattle exclusively found there, hence its name.

Helpful Hint
When buying Swiss cheeses such as Emmental and Gruyère, look for 'weeping eyes' – the holes should glisten with butterfat.

Limburger
Originated in Belgium, but today most of it is made in Germany. It is rectangular in shape with a brick-red rind and yellow, smooth-textured paste. Limburger has a pungent aroma and a strong, spicy flavour.

Helpful Hint
Strong smelling cheeses like Limburger need to be well wrapped to stop their odour overpowering other foods. The rind can be wiped with a damp cloth which will help to lessen the pungency.

Münster
German cheese with a mildly piquant flavour. It has a thin brown skin rather than rind, and smooth slightly soft white to yellow paste.

Quark
The name Quark literally means curds. It is a German, low fat soft cheese with a smooth texture and slightly acid taste.

Royalp
Also known as Swiss Tilsit. It has a rather mild flavour with a piquant aftertaste. Firm textured with a few regularly shaped holes or 'eyes'.

Sbrinz
Made only from unpasteurized milk, Sbrinz is aromatic and full flavoured.

Tilsit
This was originally made by Dutch settlers in Prussia and named after the town of Tilsit. It is easily recognized by its loaf shape and small irregular holes. The taste is piquant and mildly sour and it is sometimes flavoured with caraway seeds.

Dutch and Scandinavian Cheeses

A cheese market in Holland

Danbo
Mild-flavoured and firm-textured cheese from Denmark, sometimes flavoured with caraway seeds.

Danish Blue (Danablu)
Made with homogenized milk, Danish Blue has a sharp saltiness which diminishes as it matures. It is a white cheese with close blue veins, and a soft, slightly crumbly texture.

Edam
Edam originated in the town of Edam and is instantly

recognized by its characteristic red wax rind (although the cheeses are sold with their natural golden rind uncovered in the Netherlands). It has a smooth, slightly rubbery consistency and mild flavour which becomes stronger, drier and saltier as it ages. Today it is entirely factory made and sometimes has the addition of cumin seeds.

Gouda
Gouda is made both in the factory and farmhouse – the farmhouse product being far superior. The flavour is bland when the cheese is young but becomes more distinctive with maturity. It is golden yellow in colour with a characteristic dark yellow rind.

Havarti
A Danish cheese made in flat rounds or rectangular loaf shapes. Pale yellow in colour with numerous irregular holes, it has an aromatic, but basically bland flavour.

Jarlsberg
Norwegian cheese with a mild and buttery flavour, creamy yellow in colour with a smooth soft texture. Similar to Emmental, it too has characteristic large holes.

Jutland Blue
A high fat Danish cheese with blue-veining. It has a mature and strong flavour.

Orange Roll
A cream cheese from Denmark which is flavoured with Grand Marnier and orange and coated in chopped hazelnuts.

Samsoe
Named after the Danish island of Samsoe. It is a firm cheese made from cows' milk. It has a distinctive, mild nutty flavour.

Svenbo
Made in flat rounds or rectangular blocks, Svenbo is a fairly new hard Danish cheese. It has a characteristic sweet flavour.

Greek Cheeses

Feta
Feta may be made from ewes', goats' or cows' milk, or a mixture of these. It should always be white, moist and slightly sharp and quite salty but very refreshing.

Helpful Hint
Feta cheese should be stored in a bowl of plain or salted water or brine to keep it moist.

Haloumi
Made both with ewes' and cows' milk, Haloumi is a creamy white cheese that is soaked in brine. Often sliced and fried in oil, it should be eaten within a month or it becomes very hard.

Processed Cheese

Austrian Links
An Austrian medium fat smoked processed cheese which is made in small sausage shapes.

Bavarian Smoked
A cream coloured processed cheese, which is smoked to give added flavour. Also flavoured with pieces of ham. It is made in large sausage shapes which have a brown plastic skin and is sold in thick slices, individually wrapped.

Fondu au Raisin, Fondu aux Noix
A mild and bland French cheese which is encrusted with dried grape seeds or walnuts.

Gourmandise
A French processed cheese, pale ivory in colour, which is flavoured with hazelnut and cherry. Sold in cake form or in foil-wrapped wedges.

La Vache Qui Rit
A brand of processed cheese often referred to as 'The Laughing Cow'. It is made from Gruyère and most often sold in small foil-wrapped cubes.

Rambol Pepper
A French processed cheese-spread made from Emmental cheese and cream. It is flavoured with pepper and flamed with cognac.

Saint Julien
A French full fat processed cheese, sold in small rounds flavoured with garlic and parsley, almonds, hazelnuts and walnuts.

Swiss Petit Gruyère
Another Gruyère-based, processed cheese generally sold in boxed foil-wrapped triangles.

Soups and Starters

Hot Mozzarella

Hot Mozzarella

This is one of the simplest of Italian starters, but quite delicious. It is very important that the griddle or frying pan (skillet) is piping hot before the cheese is added, so that a golden crust forms immediately.

Metric/Imperial	*American*
350 g/12 oz Mozzarella cheese	¾ lb Mozzarella cheese
olive oil	olive oil
freshly ground pepper	freshly ground pepper
coarse salt	coarse salt
1 tablespoon chopped fresh basil	1 tablespoon chopped fresh basil
juice of 1 lemon	juice of 1 lemon

Cut the cheese into 1 cm/½ inch thick slices. Lightly grease a griddle or heavy frying pan (skillet) with oil and heat until very hot. To test that the pan is hot enough, cut off a small corner of cheese and drop into the pan. It should sizzle and colour immediately on contact with the hot oil. Add the cheese slices and as soon as they colour on the underside, flip them over with a spatula. Continue cooking until the cheese has a good crust underneath. The total cooking time will be about 3 minutes.

Broad Bean and Cheese Salad

Transfer to 4 small plates and serve immediately, sprinkled with a little extra olive oil, pepper, salt, basil and lemon juice. Serves 4.

Broad Bean and Cheese Salad

Metric/Imperial	American
1 kg/2 lb young broad beans (unshelled weight), shelled	2 lb young fava beans (unshelled weight), shelled
150 ml/¼ pint good quality green olive oil	⅔ cup good quality green olive oil
2 garlic cloves, crushed	2 garlic cloves, crushed
salt	salt
freshly ground pepper	freshly ground pepper
2 tablespoons chopped fresh sage	2 tablespoons chopped fresh sage
125 g/4 oz Pecorino cheese, crumbled	1 cup crumbled Pecorino cheese

Put the broad (fava) beans into a large bowl. Add the olive oil, garlic, salt and pepper to taste, and half the sage. Stir the dressing into the beans so that they are evenly coated. Cover the bowl with plastic wrap and chill for 2 hours.

Just before serving, stir in the crumbled cheese and sprinkle with the remaining sage. Serves 4-6.

Goats' Milk Cheese Tartlets

Metric/Imperial	American
150 g/5 oz plain flour	1¼ cups all-purpose flour
pinch of salt	pinch of salt
125 g/4 oz butter, chilled	½ cup butter, chilled
1 egg yolk	1 egg yolk
1 teaspoon water	1 teaspoon water
a little beaten egg white	a little beaten egg white
Filling:	*Filling:*
250 g/8 oz Chèvre (goats' milk cheese), rind removed	½ lb Chèvre (goats' milk cheese), rind removed
2 eggs, beaten	2 eggs, beaten
2 tablespoons brandy (optional)	2 tablespoons brandy (optional)
1 teaspoon freshly chopped thyme or ½ teaspoon dried	1 teaspoon freshly chopped thyme or ½ teaspoon dried
1 teaspoon freshly chopped marjoram or ½ teaspoon dried	1 teaspoon freshly chopped marjoram or ½ teaspoon dried
freshly ground black pepper	freshly ground black pepper

To make the pastry, sift the flour and salt into a bowl. Rub (cut) in the butter until the mixture resembles fine crumbs. Mix the egg yolk and water together, then stir into the flour mixture with a round-bladed knife until the mixture draws together. Form into a smooth ball with one hand, then chill in a refrigerator for 30 minutes.

Meanwhile, make the filling. Put the cheese into a bowl and beat with a wooden spoon until soft and creamy. Beat in the remaining ingredients with pepper to taste.

Roll out the pastry on a lightly floured board and use to line 4 loose-bottomed 10 cm/4 inch flan tins (tartlet molds) placed on a baking sheet. Prick the base of the dough in several places with a fork, then line with greaseproof (waxed) paper and fill with dried beans.

Bake the pastry cases (pie shells) 'blind' in a preheated moderately hot oven (190°C/375°F, Gas Mark 5) for 10 minutes, then remove the paper and the beans and brush the base of the dough with beaten egg white. Return to the oven and bake for 5 minutes more. Remove the sides of the tins (molds) and pour the prepared filling into the pastry cases (pie shells). Return to the oven and bake for 15 minutes until set. Serve warm. Serves 4.

Courgette (Zucchini) and Brie Cream Soup

Metric/Imperial
350 g/12 oz courgettes, sliced
3 small potatoes, peeled and quartered
1 tablespoon olive oil
salt
125 g/4 oz soft ripe Brie cheese, rind removed
freshly ground pepper
4 tablespoons double cream

American
¾ lb zucchini, sliced
3 small potatoes, peeled and quartered
1 tablespoon olive oil
salt
¼ lb soft ripe Brie cheese, rind removed
freshly ground pepper
¼ cup heavy cream

Put the courgettes (zucchini) in a large saucepan with the potatoes, oil and 1 teaspoon salt. Cover with water and stir well. Bring to the boil, lower the heat and simmer for 15 to 20 minutes until the potatoes are tender. Remove from the heat and leave to cool slightly, then strain the vegetables over a bowl. Reserve 450 ml/¾ pint (2 cups) of the stock.

Remove the courgettes (zucchini) and potatoes with a slotted spoon and place in a blender or food processor with 300 ml/½ pint (1¼ cups) of the reserved stock. Add the diced cheese and process until smooth.

Return the mixture to the rinsed-out pan and add the remaining vegetable stock. Bring to just below boiling point, stirring constantly, then add salt and pepper to taste. Pour into 4 warmed individual bowls and swirl 1 tablespoon of cream into each. Serve immediately with French bread. Serves 4.

Helpful Hint
Brie should be bought as required, but if you have to store it, wrap it in foil and place it in the warmest part of the refrigerator for the shortest possible time.

Onion Soup

Metric/Imperial	American
450 g/1 lb onions	1 lb onions
50 g/2 oz butter	¼ cup butter
25 g/1 oz flour	¼ cup flour
1.2 litres/2 pints beef stock or water	5 cups beef stock or water
salt	salt
freshly ground pepper	freshly ground pepper
75 g/3 oz Gruyère cheese or Cheddar cheese, grated	¾ cup grated Swiss cheese or Cheddar cheese

Peel and slice the onions thickly. Melt the butter over a medium heat in a large pan, add the onions and, stirring constantly, cook until transparent. Sprinkle with flour and cook until golden brown.

Remove from the heat and add the beef stock or water all at once, beat well with a whisk until the flour is incorporated, season, and return to boiling point. Reduce the heat and simmer steadily, uncovered, for 20 minutes.

To serve, pour the soup into thick earthenware bowls. Sprinkle liberally with the grated cheese and serve immediately before the cheese melts or sinks. Serves 6.

Onion Soup

Deep-fried Camembert with Cranberry Sauce

Deep-Fried Camembert with Cranberry Sauce

Metric/Imperial	American
350 g/12 oz cranberry sauce	¾ lb cranberry sauce
1 tablespoon port	1 tablespoon port
4 individual triangular portions of ripe Camembert cheese	4 individual triangular portions of ripe Camembert cheese
1 egg, beaten	1 egg, beaten
125 g/4 oz dried white breadcrumbs	1 cup dried white breadcrumbs
vegetable oil for deep-frying	vegetable oil for deep-frying
cranberry jelly, to serve	cranberry jelly, to serve

Combine the cranberry sauce and port in a bowl. Set aside.

Coat the Camembert in the beaten egg, then in the breadcrumbs, making sure that the whole cheese is thoroughly covered. Repeat with more egg and bread-crumbs if necessary. Chill in the refrigerator for 30 minutes.

Meanwhile, heat the oil in a deep-fat fryer to 190°C/375°F or until a stale bread cube turns golden brown in 30 seconds. Lower the Camembert portions gently into the hot fat then deep-fry for about 4 minutes until golden.

Remove from the fryer with a slotted spoon and drain on paper towels. Serve immediately with the cranberry sauce and garnish with spring onions (scallions) if desired. Serves 2.

Haddock and Cheese Pâté

Metric/Imperial	American
250 g/8 oz fresh haddock fillets	½ lb fresh haddock fillets
125 g/4 oz full fat soft cheese	½ cup cream cheese
1 tablespoon lemon juice	1 tablespoon lemon juice
finely grated rind of ½ lemon	finely grated rind of ½ lemon
freshly ground pepper	freshly ground pepper
lemon slices and parsley sprigs, to garnish	lemon slices and parsley sprigs, to garnish

Place the haddock in a saucepan and just cover with water. Poach the fish for 8 to 10 minutes. Drain the fish, remove the skin and flake. Leave to cool. In a large bowl, beat the cheese with the lemon juice and rind. Season with pepper and add the flaked fish. Beat until smooth and spoon into a serving dish. Garnish with lemon twists and parsley sprigs and serve with toast or crackers. Serves 4.

Prawn Cocottes

Metric/Imperial	American
25 g/1 oz butter	2 tablespoons butter
1 small onion, finely chopped	1 small onion, finely chopped
1 garlic clove, crushed	1 garlic clove, crushed
100 g/4 oz peeled prawns	½-¾ cup peeled shrimp
2 tablespoons whisky	2 tablespoons whisky
2 tablespoons full fat soft cheese, softened	2 tablespoons full fat soft cheese, softened
4 tablespoons soured cream	¼ cup sour cream
salt	salt
freshly ground pepper	freshly ground pepper
25 g/1 oz Gruyère or Emmental cheese, grated	2 tablespoons grated Swiss or Emmental cheese
a little sweet paprika or cayenne pepper	a little sweet paprika or cayenne pepper

Melt the butter in a pan, add the onion and garlic and fry gently until soft but not coloured. Add the prawns and whisky, increase the heat and fry briskly until quite dry, stirring constantly.

Remove from the heat and stir in the soft cheese, half the soured cream, a little salt and plenty of pepper. Divide equally between 2 individual cocottes, ramekins, or scallop shells. Spread the remaining soured cream over the top of the prawn mixture and sprinkle with the cheese and a little paprika or cayenne.

Bake in a preheated oven (190°C/375°F, Gas Mark 5), for 15 minutes, then put under a preheated grill for a further 2 minutes until the cheese is golden and bubbling. Serve hot as a starter with garlic bread. Serves 4.

Danish Blue Cheese Mousse

Metric/Imperial	American
300 ml/½ pint double cream, whipped	1¼ cups heavy cream, whipped
125 g/4 oz Danish Blue cheese, grated	1 cup crumbled blue cheese
125 g/4 oz Samsoe cheese, grated	1 cup grated Samsoe cheese
25 g/1 oz toasted almonds, chopped	¼ cup chopped toasted almonds
1 tablespoon gelatine, dissolved in 2 tablespoons water	1 tablespoon unflavored gelatin, dissolved in 2 tablespoons water
pinch of dry mustard	pinch of dry mustard
freshly ground pepper	freshly ground pepper
2 egg whites	2 egg whites
watercress, to garnish	watercress, to garnish

Combine the cream, cheeses and almonds in a bowl until evenly blended. Stir in the dissolved gelatine. Add the mustard and pepper to taste. Whisk the egg whites until they are stiff and then fold lightly but thoroughly into the cheese mixture.

Spoon the mousse into a 600 ml/1 pint (3 cup) ring mould and chill for at least 3 hours. Unmould carefully to serve and garnish with watercress. Serves 8.

Pastries and Pies

Spinach and Cottage Cheese Flan

Metric/Imperial	American
175 g/6 oz plain flour	1½ cups all-purpose flour
salt	salt
75 g/3 oz fat	6 tablespoons fat
cold water	cold water
Filling:	*Filling:*
5 eggs	5 eggs
50 g/2 oz butter	4 cups butter
225 g/8 oz canned or frozen spinach, or 1 lb fresh spinach, cooked, drained and chopped	8 oz canned or frozen spinach, or 1 lb fresh spinach, cooked, drained and chopped
225 g/8 oz cottage cheese	2 cups cottage cheese
salt	salt
freshly ground pepper	freshly ground pepper
¼ teaspoon ground nutmeg	¼ teaspoon ground nutmeg
150 ml/¼ pint single cream	⅔ cup light cream
25 g/1 oz Cheddar cheese, grated	2 tablespoons grated Cheddar cheese

Sift the flour and salt into a mixing bowl. Rub (cut) in the fat until the mixture resembles fine crumbs. Add enough cold water to mix to a firm dough. Knead lightly, roll out and use to line a 20 cm/8 inch flan ring placed on a baking sheet.

Line with a piece of foil and cook in a preheated oven (200°C/400°F, Gas Mark 6) for 10 minutes. Remove the foil and set the pastry case on one side. Reduce the oven temperature to 190°C/375°F, Gas Mark 5. Hard-boil (hard-cook) 2 of the eggs, shell and chop them.

Melt the butter in a saucepan, add the spinach, well drained if using canned, and heat slowly for 10 to 12 minutes if frozen, 3 to 4 minutes if canned or fresh.

Remove the saucepan from the heat, cool slightly then add the cottage cheese, hard-boiled (hard-cooked) eggs, a little salt, pepper and nutmeg. Put into the pastry case.

Beat together the remaining eggs, cream, salt and pepper and pour over the spinach mixture. Sprinkle the grated cheese on top and cook in the preheated oven for 25 to 30 minutes. Serves 4-6.

Spinach and Cottage Cheese Flan

Cheesy Calabrese Parcels

Metric/Imperial	*American*
250 g/8 oz calabrese	½ lb calabrese
salt	salt
1 × 200 g/7 oz packet frozen puff pastry, thawed	1 × ½ lb package frozen puff pastry, thawed
50 g/2 oz Cheddar cheese, grated	½ cup grated Cheddar cheese
freshly ground pepper	freshly ground pepper
beaten egg, to glaze	beaten egg, to glaze

Remove any tough or wilted leaves from the calabrese, and woody ends if necessary. Cut the tender stems into thin slices and separate the heads into florets, wash well. Cook in a saucepan of boiling salted water for about 5 minutes until just tender, drain well.

Roll out the pastry thinly and cut into eight 10 cm/4 inch squares. Divide the calabrese between the squares and sprinkle with cheese. Season to taste with salt and pepper. Brush the edges with beaten egg, fold the pastry over and pinch together to seal. Make three small slits in each parcel, arrange on a dampened baking sheet and brush with beaten egg. Bake in a preheated hot oven (220°C/ 425°F, Gas Mark 7) for 20 minutes until risen and golden. Makes 8.

Blue Cheese Country Quiche

Metric/Imperial	American
75 g/3 oz plain flour	¾ cup all-purpose flour
pinch of salt	pinch of salt
75 g/3 oz wholewheat flour	¾ cup wholewheat flour
40 g/1½ oz margarine	3 tablespoons margarine
40 g/1½ oz lard	3 tablespoons shortening
Filling:	*Filling:*
2 tablespoons oil	2 tablespoons oil
250 g/8 oz courgettes, topped, tailed and sliced	½ lb zucchini, cleaned and sliced
125 g/4 oz bacon rashers	¼ lb bacon slices
75 g/3 oz Danish Blue cheese, crumbled	½ cup crumbled blue cheese
3 eggs	3 eggs
salt	salt
freshly ground pepper	freshly ground pepper

Sift the plain flour and salt into a bowl. Stir in the whole-wheat flour. Rub (cut) in the fat until the mixture resembles fine crumbs. Mix to a stiff dough with a little cold water, then turn out on to a lightly floured board and knead lightly. Roll out and line a 20 cm/8 inch flan tin (pie pan), line with greaseproof (waxed) paper and dried beans and 'bake blind' in a preheated moderately hot oven (200°C/400°F, Gas Mark 6) for 15 minutes. Remove the paper and beans.

For the filling, heat the oil in a frying pan (skillet). Add the courgettes (zucchini) and bacon and sauté until soft. Remove from the heat and drain courgettes (zucchini) and bacon on kitchen paper towels.

Spoon the mixture into the pastry case (pie shell) and sprinkle with the cheese. In a bowl, beat the eggs and milk together and season with salt and pepper. Pour the mixture into the flan case (pie shell) and cook in a pre-heated moderately hot oven (190°C/375°F, Gas Mark 5) for 30 to 40 minutes until set. Serves 4-6.

Helpful Hint
Try to avoid storing blue cheeses in the refrigerator. The best place is under a well aerated cover in a cool dark place.

Cheese, Salami and Egg Pie

Metric/Imperial	American
6½ tablespoons olive oil	6½ tablespoons olive oil
2 medium onions, thinly sliced	2 medium onions, thinly sliced
1 garlic clove, crushed	1 garlic clove, crushed
300 g/10 oz Ricotta cheese or sieved cottage cheese	1¼ cups Ricotta cheese or sieved cottage cheese
3 hard-boiled eggs, chopped	3 hard-cooked eggs, chopped
125 g/4 oz salami, chopped	½ cup chopped salami
salt	salt
freshly ground pepper	freshly ground pepper
50 g/2 oz black olives, stoned, chopped	¼ cup pitted ripe olives, chopped
350 g/12 oz puff pastry	¾ lb puff pastry
2 tablespoons grated Parmesan cheese	2 tablespoons grated Parmesan cheese

Heat 6 tablespoons olive oil in a pan and gently sauté the onions for 5 minutes. Drain and allow to cool. Mix the onions in a large bowl with the garlic, cheese, hard-boiled (hard-cooked) eggs, salami, salt and pepper to taste, and the chopped olives.

Divide the pastry in half and roll out each piece to a circle 25 cm/10 inches in diameter. Line a 23 cm/9 inch loose-bottomed flan tin (pie pan) with one circle of the pastry. Press up the edges, and moisten with a little water or brush with beaten egg. Spread the filling over the pastry. Lay the second pastry circle over the top and pinch the edges together to seal. Score the top surface of the pastry with the point of a sharp knife. Brush with the remaining oil and sprinkle with the grated Parmesan cheese. Place in a preheated moderately hot oven (200°C/400°F, Gas Mark 6) and bake for 30 to 35 minutes until it is a rich golden brown. Serve hot, cut into wedges. Serves 6.

Helpful Hint
Salt is added to cheese during manufacture to preserve it and improve the flavour, so use salt with discretion when cooking with cheese.

Spanakopita

Spanakopita

Metric/Imperial	American
500 g/1 lb chopped cooked spinach	2 cups chopped cooked spinach
6 eggs, beaten	6 eggs, beaten
250 g/8 oz Feta cheese, crumbled	1⅓ cups crumbled Feta cheese
salt	salt
freshly ground pepper	freshly ground pepper
2 tablespoons olive oil	2 tablespoons olive oil
1 onion, finely chopped	1 onion, finely chopped
1 teaspoon dried oregano	1 teaspoon dried oregano
75 g/3 oz butter, melted	6 tablespoons butter, melted
500 g/1 lb filo pastry (see right)	1 lb filo pastry (see right)

Place the spinach in a bowl with the eggs and cheese. Mix well and add salt and pepper to taste. Heat the oil in a large saucepan and sauté the onion for about 5 minutes until soft but not coloured. Remove from the heat and add the spinach mixture and oregano, stirring well. Reserve.

Generously butter a 23×33 cm (9×13 inch) baking tin (pan). Reserve 4 sheets of filo pastry and fit the remainder into the tin (pan), buttering each sheet well. The sheets will overhang the edges of the tin (pan). Pour in the filling, then fold over the ends of the pastry sheets to cover it. Butter the reserved sheets of pastry and fold over to fit the dish. Place on top of the dish and brush with butter. Make 3 slits in the pastry with a sharp knife. Cook in a preheated moderately hot oven (190°C/375°F, Gas Mark 5) for 45 to 50 minutes until the pastry is crisp and golden brown. Cut into squares to serve. Serves 8.

Note

Filo pastry can be bought from Greek food shops and delicatessens.

Ricotta and Dill Flan

Metric/Imperial	*American*
75 g/3 oz wholewheat flour	¾ cup wholewheat flour
75 g/3 oz self-raising flour, sifted	¾ cup self-rising flour, sifted
75 g/3 oz white cooking fat or lard	6 tablespoons shortening
2-3 tablespoons water	2-3 tablespoons water
Filling:	*Filling:*
250 g/8 oz Ricotta cheese or sieved cottage cheese	1 cup Ricotta cheese or sieved cottage cheese
1 tablespoon fresh dill, chopped or 1½ teaspoons dried dill weed	1 tablespoon fresh dill, chopped or 1½ teaspoons dried dill weed
2 eggs, beaten	2 eggs, beaten
150 ml/5 fl oz single cream	⅔ cup light cream
salt	salt
freshly ground pepper	freshly ground pepper

Mix the flours together in a large bowl. Rub (cut) in the fat until the mixture resembles fine crumbs. Mix to a stiff dough with a little cold water, then turn out on to a lightly floured board and knead lightly.

Roll out the pastry and line a 20 cm/8 inch flan tin (pie pan). In a bowl, beat together the cheese, dill, eggs, cream and salt and pepper to taste. Pour into the flan case (pie shell) and cook in a preheated moderately hot oven (200°C/400°F, Gas Mark 6) for 20 minutes, then reduce to 180°C/350°F, Gas Mark 4 for 20 minutes more. Serve cold. Serves 6.

Camembert Quiche

Metric/Imperial	American
175 g/6 oz plain flour	1½ cups all-purpose flour
pinch of salt	pinch of salt
125 g/4 oz butter	½ cup butter
1 egg yolk	1 egg yolk
1 teaspoon water	1 teaspoon water
a little egg white, lightly beaten	a little egg white, lightly beaten
Filling:	*Filling:*
350 g/12 oz soft ripe Camembert cheese, rind removed	¾ lb soft ripe Camembert cheese, rind removed
2 eggs, beaten	2 eggs, beaten
150 ml/1¼ pint double cream	⅔ cup heavy cream
salt	salt
freshly ground pepper	freshly ground pepper

Sift the flour and the salt into a bowl. Rub (cut) in the fat until the mixture resembles fine crumbs. Mix the egg yolk and water together, then stir into the flour mixture with a round-bladed knife until the mixture draws together. Form into a smooth ball with one hand, then chill in the refrigerator for 30 minutes.

Roll out the dough on a lightly floured board and line a 23 cm/9 inch flan tin (pie pan), line with greaseproof (waxed) paper and dried beans and 'bake blind' in a preheated hot oven (220°C/425°F, Gas Mark 7) for 10 minutes. Remove the paper and beans and brush with the egg white. Return to the oven and bake for 5 minutes more.

Cut the cheese into small pieces and place in a heat-proof bowl. Stand the bowl in a pan of gently simmering water and heat gently, stirring constantly until the cheese has melted and is runny. Remove the bowl from the pan of water and gradually stir in the eggs and cream until evenly mixed. Add a little salt and pepper to taste.

Pour the filling into the flan case (pie shell) and cook in a preheated moderately hot oven (190°C/375°F, Gas Mark 5) for 20 minutes or until the filling is puffed up and golden brown. Serve immediately. Serves 6.

Ravioli with Ricotta and Provolone

Metric/Imperial	American
Dough:	Dough:
400 g/14 oz plain flour	3½ cups all-purpose flour
salt	salt
100 g/4 oz lard, diced	½ cup shortening, diced
2 eggs, beaten	2 eggs, beaten
juice of 1 lemon	juice of 1 lemon
Filling:	Filling:
250 g/9 oz Ricotta cheese	1 cup Ricotta cheese, firmly packed
100 g/4 oz ham, diced	½ cup diced ham
100 g/4 oz Provolone cheese, diced	½ cup diced Provolone cheese, diced
2 egg yolks	2 egg yolks
freshly ground black pepper	freshly ground black pepper
1 egg white, lightly whisked	1 egg white, lightly whisked
vegetable oil for deep-frying	vegetable oil for deep-frying

To make the dough, sift the flour and a pinch of salt on to a work surface and make a well in the centre. Add the lard (shortening), eggs and lemon juice, then work all the ingredients together to make a smooth dough.

To make the filling, press the Ricotta through a sieve (strainer) into a bowl. Add the ham, Provolone, egg yolks and salt and pepper to taste. Mix well until thoroughly combined.

Flatten the dough with a rolling pin and roll out into a fairly thin sheet. Cut out 4 circles, each one about 20 cm/ 8 inches in diameter. Divide the filling between the circles, placing it in the centre of each one. Brush the edges of the circles with a little egg white, then fold the dough over the filling to enclose it completely.

Deep-fry the ravioli one at a time in hot oil until golden brown. Drain on absorbent kitchen paper while frying the remainder. Serve hot. Serves 4.

Variation

Any leftover chopped meat can be used in place of the diced ham if desired. Chopped salted peanuts also make an interesting variation.

Savoury Breads

Samsoe Cheese Bread (Photograph: Danish Dairy Board)

Samsoe Cheese Bread

Metric/Imperial
750 g/1½ lb strong plain
   white flour
25 g/1 oz lard
½ teaspoon salt
1 × 15 g/½ oz packet 'easy
   blend' dried yeast
1 teaspoon sugar
1 teaspoon dried mixed
   herbs
1 onion, chopped
250 g/8 oz Samsoe cheese,
   grated
400 ml/⅔ pint tepid water
beaten egg, to glaze

American
6 cups white bread flour
2 tablespoons shortening
½ teaspoon salt
1 × ½ oz package 'easy
   blend' active dry yeast
1 teaspoon sugar
1 teaspoon dried mixed
   herbs
1 onion, chopped
2 cups grated Samsoe
   cheese
1¾ cups tepid water
beaten egg, to glaze

Danish Blue Ring, page 52 (Photograph: Danish Dairy Board)

Sift the flour into a warmed bowl. Rub (cut) in the lard (shortening) until the mixture resembles fine crumbs. Stir in the salt, yeast, sugar, herbs, onion and 175 g/6 oz (1½ cups) cheese. Make a well in the centre and gradually mix in enough milk to make a soft dough. Knead for 10 minutes until smooth and elastic. Leave to 'relax' for 5 minutes.

Divide the dough into 6 even-sized pieces and roll each piece into a rope about 30 cm/12 inches long. Join three of the pieces at one end and seal with a little beaten egg. Plait (braid) loosely and seal the other end as before, pressing the ropes together firmly. Repeat with remaining dough.

Put the plaits (braids) on to greased baking sheets. Cover with oiled plastic wrap and leave for about 40 minutes or until doubled in size. Brush the loaves with egg and sprinkle with the remaining cheese. Bake in a preheated hot oven (230°C/450°F, Gas Mark 8) for 20 to 25 minutes. Cool on a wire rack. Makes 2 loaves.

Danish Blue Ring

Metric/Imperial	*American*
250 g/8 oz self-raising flour	2 cups self-rising flour
1 teaspoon baking powder	1 teaspoon baking powder
50 g/2 oz butter	¼ cup butter
50 g/2 oz Danish Blue cheese, crumbled	½ cup crumbled blue cheese
about 150 ml/¼ pint milk	about ⅔ cup milk

Sift the flour and baking powder into a bowl. Rub (cut) in the butter until the mixture resembles fine crumbs. Stir in the crumbled cheese. Make a well in the centre, then, using a fork mix in enough milk to make a soft but not sticky dough. Turn on to a lightly floured board and knead until smooth. Divide the dough into 8 even-sized pieces and shape each into a ball.

Place one ball in the centre of a greased 20 cm/8 inch round cake tin (pan). Arrange the remaining balls of dough round the centre one so that they are just touching. Brush with remaining milk and bake in a moderately hot oven (200°C/400°F, Gas Mark 6) for about 25 minutes or until well risen and brown. Serves 8.

Herb Cheese Breakaway Bread

Metric/Imperial	*American*
1 French loaf	1 French loaf
125 g/4 oz full fat soft cheese with herbs and garlic	½ cup cream cheese with herbs and garlic

Slice the loaf vertically almost through to the bottom crust. Spread the cheese between the slices. Wrap the loaf tightly in foil and bake in a preheated hot oven (220°C/425°F, Gas Mark 7) for 15 minutes, then fold back the foil and bake for 5 minutes more. Remove the foil, and gently break off each piece as required. Serves 6-8.

Helpful Hint
Combine equal quantities of grated cheese and bread-crumbs for a tasty crunchy topping.

Hot Cheese and Anchovy Bread

Metric/Imperial	American
1 crusty Italian loaf	1 crusty Italian loaf
4 tablespoons olive oil	¼ cup olive oil
75 g/3 oz butter, softened	6 tablespoons butter, softened
1 garlic clove, crushed	1 garlic clove, crushed
1 × 56 g/2 oz can anchovy fillets, drained	1 × 2 oz can anchovy fillets, drained
125 g/4 oz Mozzarella, shredded	1 cup shredded Mozzarella
2 tablespoons chopped capers	2 tablespoons chopped capers

Slice the loaf in half lengthways. Combine the olive oil, butter, garlic and anchovies in a small bowl, mashing to a smooth paste. Spread this on both halves of the bread, and sprinkle the bottom half with cheese and capers. Reshape the loaf and wrap tightly in foil. Bake in a preheated hot oven (220°C/450°F, Gas Mark 7) for about 15 minutes. Serves 4-6.

Cheese and Onion Bread

Metric/Imperial	American
1 crusty French loaf	1 crusty French loaf
125 g/4 oz butter	½ cup butter
8-10 slices cheese (processed cheese, Mozzarella, Edam, Gouda, etc)	8-10 slices cheese (processed cheese, Mozzarella, Edam, Gouda, etc)
2 medium onions, thinly sliced	2 medium onions, thinly sliced
salt and pepper	salt and pepper

Slice the loaf vertically almost through to the bottom crust. Butter between the slices and over the top of the loaf. Insert a slice of cheese and a couple of onion slices between each slice and season with salt and pepper. Wrap the loaf tightly in foil and bake in a preheated hot oven (220°C/425°F, Gas Mark 7) for 10 to 15 minutes. Serves 8-10.

Macaroni Bake

Metric/Imperial	American
1 tablespoon vegetable oil	1 tablespoon vegetable oil
1 small onion, finely chopped	1 small onion, finely chopped
225 g/8 oz minced beef	½ lb minced beef
1 × 225 g/8 oz can tomatoes	1 × 8 oz can tomatoes
1 tablespoon tomato purée	1 tablespoon tomato paste
1 teaspoon dried basil	1 teaspoon dried basil
salt	salt
freshly ground pepper	freshly ground pepper
50 g/2-3 oz wholewheat macaroni	½ cup wholewheat macaroni
Cheese sauce:	*Cheese sauce:*
25 g/1 oz butter or margarine	2 tablespoons butter or margarine
25 g/1 oz plain flour	¼ cup all-purpose flour
300 ml/½ pint milk	1¼ cups milk
75 g/3 oz Cheddar cheese, grated	¾ cup grated Cheddar cheese
1 teaspoon made English mustard	1 teaspoon made English mustard
Topping:	*Topping:*
25 g/1 oz Cheddar cheese, grated	¼ cup grated Cheddar cheese
25 g/1 oz dried breadcrumbs (preferably wholemeal) or potato crisps, finely crushed	¼ cup dried breadcrumbs (preferably wholemeal) or potato crisps, finely crushed

Heat the oil in a pan, add the onion and fry gently until soft. Add the beef and fry until browned, breaking up any lumps with a wooden spoon. Stir in the tomatoes, tomato purée (paste), basil and salt and pepper to taste. Bring to the boil, stirring constantly to break up the tomatoes, then simmer for 15 minutes.

Meanwhile, cook the macaroni in boiling salted water for 15 minutes until just tender. Drain, then fold the macaroni into the meat sauce, mixing well. Turn into a casserole dish and set aside.

To make the cheese sauce, melt the butter or margarine in a pan, add the flour and cook for 2 minutes, stirring constantly. Remove from the heat and gradually add the milk, beating constantly. Return to the heat and bring to the boil, stirring then add the grated cheese, mustard and salt and pepper to taste. Simmer until thick.

Pour the cheese sauce over the meat and macaroni. Mix together the topping ingredients and sprinkle them over the cheese sauce. Bake uncovered in a preheated oven (180°C/350°F, Gas Mark 4) for 30 minutes. Serve hot with a green salad. Serves 2-4.

Macaroni Bake

Coquilles au Gratin

Metric/Imperial	American
4 scallops, opened and cleaned	4 scallops, opened and cleaned
salt	salt
freshly ground pepper	freshly ground pepper
150 ml/¼ pint dry white wine	⅔ cup dry white wine
½ onion, sliced	½ onion, sliced
1 shallot, sliced	1 shallot, sliced
bouquet garni	bouquet garni
75 g/3 oz butter	¼ cup and 2 tablespoons butter
50 g/2 oz mushrooms, finely sliced	½ cup finely sliced mushrooms
2 tomatoes, skinned, seeded and diced	2 tomatoes, skinned, seeded and diced
juice of ½ lemon	juice of ½ lemon
25 g/1 oz flour	¼ cup all-purpose flour
a little single cream	a little light cream
1 teaspoon anchovy essence	1 teaspoon anchovy essence
25 g/1 oz Gruyère cheese, grated	¼ cup grated Swiss cheese
4 tablespoons fresh white breadcrumbs	1 cup soft breadcrumbs
2 tablespoons flaked almonds, toasted	2 tablespoons slivered almonds, toasted
4 anchovy fillets, chopped	4 anchovy fillets, chopped

Scrub the scallop shells and place on a baking sheet. Rinse and dry the scallops and season them lightly with salt and pepper. Put the wine, onion, shallot and bouquet garni into a small pan. Bring to the boil and add the scallops. Reduce the heat immediately and poach for about 5 minutes – this should be enough, scallops get tougher the longer you cook them. Remove the scallops and keep warm. Strain and reserve the liquor.

Melt a third of the butter in a pan, add the mushrooms, tomatoes and lemon juice, season to taste and cook gently for about 3 minutes until the mushrooms are softened. Check the seasoning.

Melt ½ of the remaining butter in a small pan and stir in the flour. Cook for 2 to 3 minutes, remove from the heat and blend in the strained liquor from the scallops, and the mushroom mixture. Return to the heat, and stirring continuously, add enough cream to give a good coating consistency. Stir in the anchovy essence. Taste and adjust the seasoning and simmer for 5 minutes.

Cut each scallop into 4, mix with half the sauce and divide equally between the 4 scallop shells. Mix the cheese into the remaining sauce and spoon it over each shell. Sprinkle with the breadcrumbs, flake the remaining butter over and brown under a hot grill. Garnish with the almonds and anchovies. Serves 4.

Herb Cheese Pasta

Metric/Imperial	*American*
175 g/6 oz pasta shells	1½ cups pasta shells
125 g/4 oz full fat soft cheese with garlic and herbs	½ cup cream cheese with garlic and herbs
4 eggs, beaten	4 eggs, beaten
15 g/½ oz butter	1 tablespoon butter
6 bacon rashers, rinds removed and chopped	6 bacon slices, rinds removed and chopped
250 g/8 oz button mushrooms, sliced	2 cups sliced button mushrooms
1 small onion, chopped	1 small onion, chopped
tomato wedges and parsley, to garnish	tomato wedges and parsley, for garnish

Cook the pasta shells in a saucepan containing plenty of salted boiling water for 10 to 12 minutes or until tender. Drain well.

In a bowl soften the cheese and then slowly add the eggs, beating well after each addition. Set aside. Melt the butter in a saucepan and gently sauté the bacon, mushrooms and onion for 3 to 4 minutes. Add the pasta and the cheese mixture. Stir over a low heat until the mixture is well blended and the eggs have thickened slightly. Serve immediately, garnished with tomato wedges and parsley. Serves 4.

Coquilles au Gratin, page 56

Lettuce, Cheese and Ham Pancakes

Metric/Imperial	*American*
125 g/4 oz plain flour	1 cup all-purpose flour
salt	salt
1 egg	1 egg
300 ml/½ pint milk	1¼ cups milk
a little oil	a little oil
Filling:	*Filling:*
¼ iceberg lettuce, finely shredded	¼ head iceberg lettuce, finely shredded
175 g/6 oz Gruyère cheese, grated	1½ cups grated Swiss cheese
1 tablespoon grated onion	1 tablespoon grated onion
1 teaspoon French mustard	1 teaspoon Dijon mustard
2 tablespoons chopped fresh parsley	2 tablespoons chopped fresh parsley
salt	salt
freshly ground pepper	freshly ground pepper
1 egg, beaten	1 egg, beaten
8 slices cooked ham	8 slices cooked ham
150 ml/¼ pint double cream	⅔ cup heavy cream
1 tablespoon grated Parmesan cheese	1 tablespoon grated Parmesan cheese

Sift the flour and salt into a mixing bowl. Make a well in the centre and break in the egg. Gradually add the milk, stirring and gradually incorporating the flour from around the sides. When the batter is smooth, beat it well for 1 minute.

Heat an 18 cm/7 inch frying pan (skillet) and grease it lightly with a little oil. When the pan is thoroughly hot, pour in enough batter to thinly coat the base. Cook over moderate heat until golden brown underneath, then turn the pancake over and cook the other side. Make 7 more pancakes in the same way, lightly greasing the pan after every third pancake. Keep the pancakes warm in a folded tea towel (dish towel).

For the filling, place the shredded lettuce in a bowl. Reserve 2 tablespoons of the Gruyère (Swiss) cheese and mix the remainder with the lettuce. Add the grated onion.

In another bowl blend the mustard with the parsley, salt and pepper to taste and the egg. Add the egg mixture to the lettuce and cheese and stir well.

Top each pancake with a slice of ham. Divide the lettuce and cheese filling between the pancakes and roll them up. Arrange the pancakes in a shallow ovenproof dish. Pour over the cream and sprinkle with the reserved Gruyère (Swiss) cheese and Parmesan. Bake in a preheated moderately hot oven (190°C/375°F, Gas Mark 5) for 20 minutes. Serve at once. Serves 4.

Camembert Croquettes

Metric/Imperial	American
1 × 250 g/8 oz ripe Camembert, crust removed	1 × ½ lb ripe Camembert, crust removed
40 g/1½ oz butter	3 tablespoons butter
40 g/1½ oz plain flour	¼ cup plus 2 tablespoons all-purpose flour
150 ml/¼ pint milk	⅔ cup milk
salt	salt
freshly ground pepper	freshly ground pepper
50 g/2 oz cooked lean ham, chopped	¼ cup chopped cooked lean ham
flour for coating	flour for coating
1 egg, beaten	1 egg, beaten
breadcrumbs, for coating	breadcrumbs, for coating
vegetable oil for frying	vegetable oil for frying
sprigs of parsley, to garnish	sprigs of parsley, to garnish

Dice the Camembert. Melt the butter in a saucepan, stir in the flour and cook for 1 minute, stirring constantly. Remove from the heat and gradually stir in the milk. Return to the heat and bring to the boil, stirring. Add the salt and pepper, cheese and ham immediately. Spoon the cheese mixture on to a plate, cover and leave until completely cold.

Using floured hands, divide the mixture into 8 equal portions and roll into small sausage shapes. Coat the croquettes evenly in flour, egg and breadcrumbs.

Heat the oil in a frying pan (skillet) and shallow fry the croquettes, a few at a time, for 4 to 5 minutes, turning, until golden brown and crisp. Drain on kitchen paper towels. Serve at once garnished with parsley. Serves 4.

Variation

Nutty Cheese Croquettes Replace the Camembert cheese and ham with 4 chopped hard-boiled (hard-cooked) eggs, 1 teaspoon chopped parsley, 125 g/4 oz (1 cup) grated Cheddar cheese and 50 g/2 oz (¼ cup) crushed salted peanuts.

Helpful Hint

When ripe, Camembert should be just bulging from the crust. Avoid over-ripe Camembert as it tastes bitter.

Cheese Kebabs on Savoury Rice

Metric/Imperial	American
Savoury rice:	Savoury rice:
25 g/1 oz butter	2 tablespoons butter
1 onion, chopped	1 onion, chopped
1 garlic clove, crushed	1 garlic clove, crushed
250 g/8 oz long-grain rice	1 cup plus 2 tablespoons long-grain rice
600 ml/1 pint chicken stock	2½ cups chicken stock
1 teaspoon tomato purée	1 teaspoon tomato paste
salt	salt
freshly ground pepper	freshly ground pepper
125 g/4 oz frozen peas	⅔ cup frozen peas
75 g/3 oz Cheddar cheese or Parmesan cheese, grated	⅓ cup grated Cheddar cheese or Parmesan cheese
Kebabs:	Kebabs:
4 rashers streaky bacon, rinds removed and halved	4 slices fatty bacon, rinds removed and halved
75 g/3 oz Gruyère or Cheddar cheese, cut into chunks	3 oz Swiss or Cheddar cheese, cut into chunks
250 g/8 oz sausages, halved	½ lb sausage links, halved
125 g/4 oz button mushrooms, wiped	1 cup button mushrooms, wiped
4 tomatoes, halved	4 tomatoes, halved
vegetable oil for brushing	vegetable oil for brushing

Melt the butter in a saucepan, add the onion and garlic and sauté, stirring until soft but not brown. Add the rice and continue cooking and stirring over a moderate heat until it turns a pale gold colour. Pour the stock into the pan and add the tomato purée (paste), salt and pepper to taste, and the peas. Cover and simmer gently for 20 minutes until the stock is absorbed and the rice is tender. Stir in the cheese.

For the kebabs, wrap the bacon around the cheese and thread on to 8 skewers alternating with the other ingredients. Brush all over lightly with oil and place under a preheated moderate grill for 10 to 15 minutes, turning once. Serve on the hot savoury rice. Serves 4.

Cheese Soufflé

Metric/Imperial	American
40 g/1½ oz butter	3 tablespoons butter
3 tablespoons flour	3 tablespoons flour
250 ml/8 fl oz warm milk	1 cup warm milk
40 g/1½ oz Parmesan cheese, freshly grated	⅓ cup freshly grated Parmesan cheese
salt	salt
freshly ground pepper	freshly ground pepper
pinch of cayenne pepper	pinch of cayenne pepper
pinch of grated nutmeg	pinch of grated nutmeg
4 egg yolks	4 egg yolks
5 egg whites	5 egg whites
½ teaspoon cream of tartar	½ teaspoon cream of tartar

Butter a 20 cm/8 inch soufflé dish and place on a baking sheet.

Melt the butter in a saucepan, stir in the flour and cook over low heat for 1 minute. Remove from the heat, cool slightly, then blend in the milk, stirring until smooth. Return to the heat and stir until boiling, then remove from the heat and stir in the cheese and seasonings. Beat in the egg yolks, 1 at a time. Whisk the egg whites with the cream of tartar until firm but not brittle, and fold into the cheese mixture.

Pour the mixture into the prepared dish (see Helpful Hint). Immediately place the soufflé dish in a preheated moderately hot oven (190°C/375°F, Gas Mark 5). Bake the soufflé until it is well risen, golden brown on top and just firm, about 25 minutes. Serve at once. Serves 4.

Variation

Stir in leftover chopped chicken or ham, or peeled prawns (shelled shrimp) with the cheese. Mix thoroughly.

Helpful Hint

The appearance of a soufflé is all important. To expel any air pockets in the mixture before baking, tap the bottom of the soufflé dish lightly on the work surface. The soufflé will rise evenly in a 'crown' if you smooth the top of the mixture and then cut a spoon quickly around the surface about 2.5 cm/1 inch from the edge.

Cheese Soufflé

Herby Cheese Omelette

Metric/Imperial	American
2 eggs, separated	2 eggs, separated
1 tablespoon water	1 tablespoon water
1 teaspoon mixed herbs	1 teaspoon mixed herbs
salt	salt
freshly ground pepper	freshly ground pepper
15 g/½ oz butter	1 tablespoon butter
25 g/1 oz Edam cheese, grated	¼ cup grated Edam cheese

Beat the egg yolks in a bowl with the water, herbs and seasoning to taste. Whisk the egg whites until stiff and fold into the egg yolk mixture.

Melt the butter in an 18 to 20 cm/7 to 8 inch omelette pan, pour in the mixture and cook over low heat until lightly set and golden brown underneath. Sprinkle with grated cheese and place under a preheated high grill (broiler) until the top puffs and turns golden. Fold the omelette in half and serve immediately. Serves 1.

Croque Monsieur

Metric/Imperial	*American*
8 thin slices white bread	8 thin slices white bread
75 g/3 oz butter	¼ cup plus 2 tablespoons butter
4 slices lean cooked ham	4 slices lean cooked ham
125 g/4 oz Cheddar cheese, grated	1 cup grated Cheddar cheese
butter or oil for frying	butter or oil for frying

Butter the bread and make 4 sandwiches with the ham
and cheese, pressing firmly together. Trim off the crusts.
Cut each sandwich into 3 fingers. Fry the bread fingers in
shallow hot fat or butter until golden brown on both sides.
Drain on absorbent kitchen paper and serve hot. Serves 4.

Welsh Rarebit

Metric/Imperial	*American*
15 g/½ oz butter	1 tablespoon butter
1 tablespoon plain flour	1 tablespoon all-purpose flour
2 tablespoons milk	2 tablespoons milk
4 tablespoons brown ale or dark beer	¼ cup brown ale or dark beer
2 teaspoons Worcestershire sauce	2 teaspoons Worcestershire sauce
1 teaspoon made English mustard	1 teaspoon prepared English mustard
½ teaspoon salt	½ teaspoon salt
½ teaspoon freshly ground pepper	½ teaspoon freshly ground pepper
250 g/8 oz Cheddar cheese, grated	2 cups grated Cheddar cheese
4 slices hot buttered toast	4 slices hot buttered toast

Melt the butter in a saucepan. Remove from the heat and
stir in the flour to make a smooth paste. Gradually stir in the
milk, ale, Worcestershire sauce, mustard, salt and pepper.
Return to low heat and cook, stirring constantly, for 2 to 3
minutes or until the mixture is thick and smooth. Add the

cheese and cook, stirring constantly until the cheese has melted.

Place the toast on 4 flameproof serving plates. Divide the cheese mixture between the slices. Place under a pre-heated grill (broiler) for 3 to 4 minutes or until golden brown. Serve at once. Serves 4.

Variation

Yorkshire Rarebit Add a thick slice of lean cooked ham to the top of each Rarebit and place under a preheated grill (broiler) for 3 to 4 minutes. Remove from the heat and place a hot poached egg on each piece of ham. Serve at once.

Courgette (Zucchini) Cheese and Bacon Bake

Metric/Imperial	American
1 kg/2 lb small, firm courgettes, sliced into rings	2 lb small, firm zucchini, sliced into rings
4 eggs	4 eggs
450 ml/¾ pint milk	2 cups milk
250 g/8 oz mature Cheddar cheese, grated	2 cups grated sharp Cheddar cheese
salt	salt
freshly ground pepper	freshly ground pepper
pinch of paprika	pinch of paprika
75 g/3 oz streaky bacon, lightly grilled	4 slices fatty bacon, lightly broiled

Place the courgettes (zucchini) in a saucepan, cover with boiling water and blanch for 2 minutes, then drain them in a colander and allow to cool.

Beat the eggs in a bowl with the milk and stir in 150 g/ 5 oz (1¼ cups) cheese. Add salt, pepper and paprika to taste and set aside.

Lightly butter a 1.2 litre/2 pint (5 cup) gratin dish and layer the courgettes (zucchini) and bacon to within 1 cm (½ inch) of the top. Pour over the egg mixture and sprinkle with the remaining cheese. Bake in a preheated moderate oven (180°C/350°F, Gas Mark 4) for 40 to 45 minutes until the cheese mixture is set and the cheese on top is melted and golden brown. Serves 6.

Vegetables and Salads

Baked Fennel with Cheese Sauce

Metric/Imperial	American
450 ml/¾ pint milk	2 cups milk
1 slice onion	1 slice onion
1 small stick celery	1 small stalk celery
3 peppercorns	3 peppercorns
1 bay leaf	1 bay leaf
pinch of grated nutmeg	pinch of grated nutmeg
50 g/2 oz butter	¼ cup butter
3 tablespoons plain flour	3 tablespoons all-purpose
salt	flour
freshly ground pepper	salt
4 small heads fennel	freshly ground pepper
juice of ½ lemon	4 small heads fennel
50 g/2 oz chopped Parma ham	juice of ½ lemon
3 tablespoons grated Parmesan cheese	¼ cup chopped Parma ham
	3 tablespoons grated Parmesan cheese

In a small heavy saucepan, heat the milk with the vegetables, peppercorns, bay leaf and nutmeg until it bubbles around the edge. Remove from the heat, stand for 20 minutes, then strain, reserving the milk and discarding the vegetables, bay leaf and peppercorns.

Wipe out the saucepan and melt the butter in it. Remove from the heat, blend in the flour and stir over a low heat for 1 minute. Add the milk slowly and stir until smooth. Season with salt and pepper. Stir over moderate heat until boiling, then lower the heat and cook for 3 minutes more.

Meanwhile prepare the fennel. Trim off the feathery pieces from the top of each head of fennel and reserve. Remove any brown patches from the fennel with a potato peeler. Cut the fennel into wedges or thick slices and drop into a saucepan of boiling salted water, with the lemon juice. Cook for 15 minutes until just tender — test with the tip of a sharp knife. Drain the fennel and put into a shallow ovenproof dish.

Add the ham and 2 tablespoons Parmesan cheese to the warm sauce. Spoon evenly over the fennel and sprinkle with the remaining cheese. Place in a preheated moderately hot oven (190°C/375°F, Gas Mark 5) for 10 to 15 minutes until lightly golden. Garnish with the feathery fennel tops and serve hot. Serves 4.

Cheesy Layered Potatoes

Metric/Imperial	American
50 g/2 oz butter, softened	¼ cup butter, softened
750 g/1½ lb potatoes, thinly sliced	1½ lb potatoes, thinly sliced
¼ teaspoon ground nutmeg	¼ teaspoon ground nutmeg
salt	salt
freshly ground pepper	freshly ground pepper
125 g/4 oz Cheddar cheese, grated	1 cup grated Cheddar cheese
450 ml/¾ pint milk	2 cups milk
150 ml/¼ pint single cream	⅔ cup light cream

Butter a 1.2 litre/2 pint (5 cup) gratin dish, and cover the base with a layer of overlapping potato slices. Dot with butter, sprinkle with a little nutmeg, salt and pepper and cheese. Repeat these layers until the ingredients are used up, finishing with a layer of cheese.

Mix together the milk and cream and pour into the dish, taking care not to disturb the cheese.

Cook in a preheated moderate oven (180°C/350°F, Gas Mark 4) for 1½ hours, or until the potatoes are tender and the topping browned. Serves 6.

Cheesy Layered Potatoes

Courgettes (Zucchini) with Cheese and Cream

Metric/Imperial	American
50 g/2 oz butter	¼ cup butter
1 medium onion, thinly sliced	1 medium onion, thinly sliced
450 g/1 lb courgettes, sliced	1 lb zucchini, sliced
2 eggs	2 eggs
300 ml/½ pint double cream	1¼ cups heavy cream
grated nutmeg	grated nutmeg
salt	salt
freshly ground black pepper	freshly ground black pepper
50 g/2 oz Gruyère cheese, grated	½ cup grated Swiss cheese

Melt ½ the butter in a large frying pan (skillet), add the onion and sauté gently until soft. Remove with a slotted spoon and place in a buttered ovenproof dish. Melt the remaining butter in the pan, add the courgette (zucchini) slices and sauté for about 10 minutes until golden brown on both sides, turning frequently. Transfer to the dish and mix with the onions.

In a bowl, whisk the eggs well to mix, then beat in the cream, nutmeg, and salt and pepper to taste. Pour over the courgettes (zucchini) and onions, then sprinkle the cheese evenly over the top.

Bake uncovered in a preheated moderately hot oven (200°C/400°F, Gas Mark 6) for 20 to 25 minutes or until the custard is set and the topping is golden and bubbling. Serve hot. Serves 4.

Camembert à la Ritz

Metric/Imperial	American
1 × 250 g/8 oz round Camembert	1 × 8 oz round Camembert
25 g/1 oz chopped apple	¼ cup chopped apple
25 g/1 oz chopped celery	¼ cup chopped celery
25 g/1 oz chopped walnuts	¼ cup chopped walnuts

Remove the top crust of the Camembert and using a spoon scoop out the cheese, leaving the shell intact. Cut the Camembert into small cubes. Gently mix the Camembert, apple, celery and walnuts together until blended. Pile the mixture back into the Camembert shell. Serves 4.

Crispy Cauliflower Cheese

Metric/Imperial	American
1 cauliflower	1 cauliflower
salt	salt
50 g/2 oz butter	¼ cup butter
175 g/6 oz bacon rashers, chopped	9 bacon slices, chopped
25 g/1 oz plain flour	¼ cup all-purpose flour
450 ml/¾ pint milk	2 cups milk
175 g/6 oz Cheddar cheese, grated	1½ cups grated Cheddar cheese
freshly ground pepper	freshly ground pepper
2 tablespoons fresh breadcrumbs	2 tablespoons soft bread crumbs
parsley, to garnish	parsley, to garnish

Trim the green leaves of the cauliflower, core and wash well. Place stalk side down in a saucepan of boiling salted water and simmer for 15 minutes, or until just tender when tested with a skewer (be sure not to overcook). Drain and place in a flameproof dish.

Meanwhile melt the butter in a saucepan. Add the bacon and sauté gently for 5 minutes, then add the mushrooms and sauté for 3 minutes more. Remove from the heat, blend in the flour, then return to a low heat, stirring for 1 minute.

Again remove from the heat and gradually stir in the milk. Return the pan to the heat and stir constantly until the sauce thickens; simmer for 3 minutes.

Stir in 125 g/4 oz (1 cup) cheese and salt and pepper to taste. Pour the sauce over the cauliflower. Mix the remaining cheese and breadcrumbs together and sprinkle over the cauliflower. Place under a preheated hot grill (broiler) until the cheese has melted and is golden brown. Garnish with parsley. Serves 4.

Feta Salad

Metric/Imperial	American
4 tomatoes, quartered	4 tomatoes, quartered
1 large cucumber, peeled and sliced	1 large cucumber, pared and sliced
1 medium onion, thinly sliced	1 medium onion, thinly sliced
125 g/4 oz Feta cheese, broken into chunks	2/3 cup Feta cheese, broken into chunks
12-16 black olives	12-16 ripe olives
Dressing:	*Dressing:*
4 tablespoons olive oil	1/4 cup olive oil
2 tablespoons lemon juice	2 tablespoons lemon juice
1 garlic clove, crushed	1 garlic clove, crushed
salt	salt
freshly ground pepper	freshly ground pepper
1 tablespoon chopped fresh basil and oregano	1 tablespoon chopped fresh basil and oregano

Place the salad ingredients in a bowl. For the dressing, combine all the ingredients in a screw-top jar. Shake until the mixture is pale and smooth, then pour over the salad. Toss well and serve. Serves 4-6.

Feta Salad

Chef's Salad (Photograph: Danish Dairy Board)

Chef's Salad

Metric/Imperial	*American*
250 g/8 oz gammon, cooked and cut into thick strips	½ lb cooked ham, cut into thick strips
125 g/4 oz Danish Blue cheese, diced	¼ lb blue cheese, diced
½ Cos lettuce, shredded	½ head Romaine lettuce, shredded
1 bunch radishes, trimmed	1 bunch radishes, trimmed
5 cm/2 inch piece cucumber, sliced	2 inch piece cucumber, sliced
1 onion, sliced into rings	1 onion, sliced into rings
Dressing:	*Dressing:*
pinch of dry mustard	pinch of dry mustard
salt	salt
freshly ground pepper	freshly ground pepper
pinch sugar	pinch sugar
4 tablespoons oil	¼ cup oil
2 tablespoons wine vinegar	2 tablespoons wine vinegar

Arrange the salad ingredients in alternate layers in a glass bowl.

For the dressing, place all the ingredients in a screw-top jar and shake until well mixed. Spoon over the salad just before serving. Serves 3-4.

Summer Salad

Metric/Imperial	American
1 small lettuce, separated into leaves	1 small head lettuce, separated into leaves
1 small head celery, chopped	1 small head celery, chopped
125 g/4 oz Gouda cheese, cubed	¼ lb Gouda cheese, cubed
125 g/4 oz ham, cubed	½ cup diced cooked ham
50 g/2 oz raisins	⅓ cup raisins
1 tablespoon chopped fresh parsley	1 tablespoon chopped fresh parsley
½ bunch radishes, trimmed and sliced	½ bunch radishes, trimmed and sliced
radish roses, to garnish	radish roses, for garnish
Sour Cream Dressing:	*Sour Cream Dressing:*
150 ml/¼ pint soured cream	⅔ cup sour cream
salt	salt
freshly ground black pepper	freshly ground black pepper
½ teaspoon Tabasco	½ teaspoon hot pepper sauce
¼ teaspoon dried thyme	¼ teaspoon dried thyme
¼ teaspoon dried oregano	¼ teaspoon dried oregano
½ teaspoon Worcestershire sauce	½ teaspoon Worcestershire sauce

Wash the lettuce leaves thoroughly, and dry by patting with kitchen paper towels. Tear them into pieces and line 4 individual salad bowls. Mix the remaining salad ingredients together. Combine all the dressing ingredients in a screw-top jar and shake well. Pour over the salad and toss. Arrange the tossed salad over the lettuce and garnish with radishes. Serves 4 as a main course.

Helpful Hint
To make a radish rose, trim the stalk to about 1 cm/½ inch. Cut a deep zig-zag line around the centre of the radish and gently ease the 2 halves apart. This will give you 2 flower-shaped pieces. Make these just before serving as the cut surfaces discolour quickly.

Ankara Salad

Metric/Imperial	American
½ small cauliflower	½ small cauliflower
125 g/4 oz Gouda cheese, cubed	¼ lb Gouda cheese, cubed
1 × 227 g/8 oz can pineapple cubes, drained	1 × 8 oz can pineapple cubes, drained
50 g/2 oz raisins	⅓ cup raisins
1 tablespoon chopped fresh parsley	1 tablespoon chopped fresh parsley
Sour Cream Dressing (page 72)	Sour Cream Dressing (page 72)
4 slices rye bread	4 slices rye bread
To garnish:	For garnish:
sliced rings of red pepper	sliced rings of red pepper
paprika	paprika

Combine the salad ingredients in a large bowl with the dressing. Pile on to the rye bread and serve garnished with the red pepper and sprinkled with paprika. Serves 4.

Cheese Stuffed Mushrooms

Metric/Imperial	American
24 mushroom caps	24 mushroom caps
25 g/1 oz butter	2 tablespoons butter
salt	salt
3 tablespoons capers	3 tablespoons capers
175 g/6 oz Roquefort cheese, crumbled	1½ cups crumbled Roquefort cheese

Wipe the mushrooms, remove the stalks and chop finely. Put the mushroom caps into a lightly greased ovenproof dish. Melt the butter in a saucepan and sauté the mushroom stalks for 5 minutes. Season to taste with salt and stir in the capers. Spoon the filling into the mushrooms. Sprinkle over the cheese and bake in a preheated moderately hot oven (190°C/375°F, Gas Mark 5) for about 15 minutes or until the mushrooms are tender and the cheese is lightly browned. Serves 6.

Cheesecakes and Desserts

Swiss-style Cheesecake

Swiss-style Cheesecake

Metric/Imperial
Cheesecake filling:
15 g/½ oz powdered
  gelatine
3 tablespoons lemon juice
225 g/8 oz cottage cheese
100 g/4 oz full fat soft
  cheese
finely grated rind of ½
  lemon
2 eggs, separated
100 g/4 oz caster sugar
150 ml/5 fl oz double cream
50-75 g/2-3 oz raisins
Sponge cake:
75 g/3 oz plain flour
1 level teaspoon baking
  powder
¼ teaspoon salt
3 egg yolks
75 g/3 oz caster sugar
4 tablespoons boiling water
1 teaspoon vanilla essence
1 teaspoon finely grated
  lemon rind
lemon curd or apricot jam
sifted icing sugar

American
Cheesecake filling:
1 envelope unflavored
  gelatin
3 tablespoons lemon juice
1 cup cottage cheese
½ cup package cream
  cheese
finely grated rind of ½
  lemon
2 eggs, separated
½ cup sugar
⅔ cup heavy cream
½ cup raisins
Sponge cake:
¾ cup all-purpose flour
1 level teaspoon baking
  powder
¼ teaspoon salt
3 egg yolks
6 tablespoons sugar
4 tablespoons boiling water
1 teaspoon vanilla extract
1 teaspoon finely grated
  lemon rind
lemon curd or apricot jam
sifted confectioners' sugar

Place the gelatine in a cup and stir in the lemon juice and 3 tablespoons cold water. Leave aside for 5 minutes to swell, then place the cup in a pan of hot water and heat gently until the gelatine melts. Cool slightly.

Sieve the cottage cheese through a metal sieve into a bowl and add the soft cheese, lemon rind and egg yolks. Mix together and stir in the gelatine (alternatively, to save sieving the cottage cheese, use a food processor to blend ingredients together).

Whisk the egg whites until very stiff then add the sugar gradually, whisking well after each addition. Whip the cream until softly stiff. Fold the cream, raisins and then the whisked egg whites into the gelatine mixture until evenly blended.

Turn the cheesecake mixture into a lightly oiled 20 cm/8 inch springform cake tin and refrigerate for several hours until firmly set.

Meanwhile make the sponge cake: preheat the oven to 180°C/350°F/Gas 4, shelf above centre. Grease and line a 20 cm/8 inch sandwich tin.

Sift the flour with the baking powder and salt. Whisk the egg yolks in a large bowl until very thick, foamy and mousse-like. Then, whisking, add the caster sugar a tablespoon at a time; whisk well after each addition until the mixture is pale and thick.

Carefully mix in the water, vanilla essence and lemon rind, then gently fold in the flour mixture until evenly blended.

Spread the cake mixture in the prepared tin and bake for about 25 minutes until it is well risen and firm to a light touch. Leave the cake in the tin to cool for about 10 minutes then turn out on to a wire rack and leave until cold. Cut the cake in half; place each layer, cut side up, on a worktop and spread fairly thickly with lemon curd or apricot jam.

Remove the set cheesecake from the tin and sandwich between the sponge layers. Dust the top very thickly with icing (confectioners') sugar and, using the back of a long knife, mark a trellis pattern in the sugar. Serves 8-10.

Variation

Stir some roughly chopped hazelnuts into the cheesecake filling with the raisins.

Hazelnut Cheesecake

Metric/Imperial	*American*
125 g/4 oz butter or margarine	½ cup butter or margarine
125 g/4 oz soft brown sugar	⅔ cup soft brown sugar
175 g/6 oz digestive biscuits, finely crushed	1 cup finely crushed Graham crackers
50 g/2 oz ground hazelnuts	½ cup ground hazelnuts
Filling:	*Filling:*
125 g/4 oz nut brittle	¼ lb nut brittle
450 g/1 lb full fat soft cheese	2 cups cream cheese
250 g/8 oz caster sugar	1 cup sugar
4 eggs, separated	4 eggs, separated
few drops of vanilla essence	few drops of vanilla extract
300 ml/½ pint double or whipping cream	1¼ cups heavy or whipping cream
3 tablespoons gelatine	3 tablespoons unflavored gelatin
120 ml/4 fl oz water	½ cup water
75 g/3 oz shelled hazelnuts, flaked	¾ cup shelled hazelnuts, slivered
Topping:	*Topping:*
75 g/3 oz shelled hazelnuts	¾ cup shelled hazelnuts
125 g/4 oz plain chocolate, broken into pieces	4 squares semisweet chocolate, broken into pieces

Melt the butter with the brown sugar in a saucepan over gentle heat and stir in the biscuit (cracker) crumbs with the ground hazelnuts. Press evenly over the bottom of greased 25 to 30 cm/10 to 12 inch round spring-release tin (spring-form pan). Chill.

Crush the nut brittle finely with a rolling pin. Soften the cheese in a large mixing bowl. Beat in 125 g/4 oz (½ cup) caster sugar, the egg yolks, vanilla and cream. Put the gelatine and water into a small heatproof bowl over a saucepan of hot water and stir until the gelatine has dissolved. Beat this into the cheese mixture, and leave on one side until the mixture is on the point of setting.

Whisk the egg whites until stiff, then whisk in the remaining caster sugar. Fold lightly but thoroughly into the cheese mixture, together with the crushed nut brittle and the flaked (slivered) hazelnuts. Spoon the mixture into the prepared tin (pan) and shake gently to level the surface. Chill for 3 to 4 hours or until set.

Meanwhile, prepare the topping. Spread out the whole hazelnuts on a freezerproof plate and freeze for 20 minutes. Melt the chocolate in a heatproof bowl over a saucepan of hot water. Stir the shelled hazelnuts into the melted chocolate so that they are evenly coated. Lift the hazelnuts out and place in small clusters on a sheet of greased greaseproof (waxed) paper. Remove the cheese-cake from the tin (pan) carefully. Decorate with clusters of chocolate-coated hazelnuts. Serves 10-12.

Frozen Lemon Cheesecake

Metric/Imperial	American
250 g/8 oz full fat soft cheese	1 cup cream cheese
125 g/4 oz caster sugar	½ cup sugar
grated rind and juice of 2 lemons	grated rind and juice of 2 lemons
2 egg yolks	2 egg yolks
300 ml/½ pint double or whipping cream, whipped	1¼ cups heavy or whipping cream, whipped
To decorate:	To decorate:
small mint leaves	small mint leaves
whisked egg white	whisked egg white
caster sugar	superfine sugar

Soften the cheese in a mixing bowl. Beat in the caster (superfine) sugar, lemon rind and juice and the egg yolks. Fold in the whipped cream. Spoon into a dampened metal 'bombe' mould, or a freezerproof jelly mould (gelatin mold). Put into the freezer until quite firm and frozen.

Meanwhile, prepare the decoration: Dip the mint leaves into the whisked egg white, then dust evenly with caster (superfine) sugar. Allow to dry at room temperature.

Carefully unmould the frozen lemon cheesecake on to a serving dish and decorate with the frosted mint leaves. Serve immediately. Serves 4-6.

Maraschino Cherry Cheesecake

Maraschino Cherry Cheesecake

Metric/Imperial
100 g/4 oz butter or
  margarine
100 g/4 oz caster sugar
175 g/6 oz digestive
  biscuits, finely crushed
50 g/2 oz blanched
  almonds, chopped
Filling:
1 × 225 g/8 oz jar
  maraschino cherries
450 g/1 lb full fat soft
  cheese
225 g/8 oz caster sugar
4 eggs, separated
300 ml/½ pint soured
  cream
30 g/1 oz powdered
  gelatine
Topping:
450 ml/¾ pint double or
  whipping cream,
  whipped
12 maraschino cherries on
  stems
75 g/3 oz split almonds,
  toasted

American
½ cup butter or margarine
½ cup sugar
1½ cups finely crushed
  Graham crackers
½ cup chopped almonds
Filling:
1 × 8 oz jar maraschino
  cherries
2 cups package cream
  cheese
1 cup sugar
4 eggs, separated
1¼ cups sour cream
2 envelopes unflavored
  gelatin
Topping:
1¾ cups heavy or
  whipping cream,
  whipped
12 maraschino cherries on
  stems
½ cup split almonds,
  toasted

Melt the butter or margarine and sugar in a saucepan over a gentle heat and stir in the biscuit crumbs with the chopped almonds. Press evenly over the bottom of a greased, loose-bottomed 25 to 30 cm/10 to 12 inch round cake tin. Chill while you make the filling.

Drain the maraschino cherries, reserving the syrup. Roll the cherries on kitchen paper to absorb excess moisture. Soften the cheese in a large mixing bowl. Beat in half of the sugar, the egg yolks and soured cream. Put the gelatine and 8 tablespoons of the maraschino syrup (adding a little water, if necessary) into a small heatproof bowl over a saucepan of hot water and stir until the gelatine has dissolved. Beat the gelatine into the cheese mixture. Leave on one side until on the point of setting.

Whisk the egg whites until stiff, then whisk in the remaining caster sugar. Fold lightly but thoroughly into the cheese mixture, together with the maraschino cherries. Spoon into the tin and chill for 3 to 4 hours or until set.

Ease the sides of the tin carefully away from the cheesecake and lift the set cheesecake out on the tin base. Pipe the whipped cream on top of the cheesecake and decorate with stemmed maraschino cherries and toasted almonds. Serves 10-12.

Coeur à la Crème, page 80

Coeur à la Crème

Metric/Imperial	American
250 g/8 oz cottage cheese	1 cup cottage cheese
1 teaspoon salt	1 teaspoon salt
300 ml/½ pint double or whipping cream, lightly whipped	1¼ cups heavy or whipping cream, lightly whipped
To serve:	To serve:
300 ml/½ pint double or whipping cream	1¼ cups heavy or whipping cream
berry fruits	berry fruits
granulated sugar	sugar

Rinse 4 to 6 small heart-shaped moulds in cold water. Alternatively use clean empty yogurt cartons, the bottoms pierced with a few holes. Put the cottage cheese into a clean piece of muslin (cheesecloth) and squeeze to remove as much excess moisture as possible. Put the cheese into a bowl with the salt and work together. Press the cheese through a sieve into a bowl and stir in the cream.

Spoon the mixture into the moulds and stand them on a tray to catch any liquid. Chill for 6 hours.

Unmould on to a serving dish. Spoon a little cream over each coeur and serve with a bowl of strawberries or raspberries, and sugar. Serves 4-6.

Mon Ami

Metric/Imperial	American
2 egg yolks	2 egg yolks
50 g/2 oz caster sugar	¼ cup sugar
125 g/4 oz full fat soft cheese	½ cup cream cheese
2 tablespoons honey	2 tablespoons honey
grated rind and juice of ½ lemon	grated rind and juice of ½ lemon
300 ml/¼ pint double or whipping cream, whipped	⅔ cup heavy or whipped cream, whipped
angelica leaves, to decorate	angelica leaves, to decorate

Put the egg yolks and caster sugar into a heatproof bowl over a saucepan of hot water and whisk until the mixture is thick, light and creamy. Soften the cheese in a mixing bowl and beat in the honey, lemon rind and juice and the whisked egg and sugar mixture. Allow to cool.

Fold the whipped cream into the cheese mixture. Spoon into stemmed glasses and chill. Decorate with angelica leaves and serve with sponge fingers (lady fingers) and wafers. Serves 4-6.

Fan-shaped Pastries

Metric/Imperial	American
350 g/12 oz puff pastry	¾ lb puff pastry
2 teaspoons caster sugar	2 teaspoons sugar
1 egg white, lightly whisked	1 egg white, lightly whisked
icing sugar to dust	confectioners' sugar to dust
Filling:	Filling:
125 g/4 oz Ricotta cheese	½ cup Ricotta cheese
2 tablespoons caster sugar	2 tablespoons sugar
150 ml/¼ pint double or whipping cream, whipped	⅔ cup heavy or whipping cream, whipped
4 tablespoons chopped glacé fruit	4 tablespoons chopped candied fruit

Roll out the pastry thinly. Using an 18 cm/7 inch tea-plate as a guide, cut out 4 circles. Cut each circle in quarters to give 16 equal sections. Trim the rounded side of each pastry section with a pastry wheel. Place on a lightly greased baking sheet and chill for 30 minutes.

Bake in a preheated moderately hot oven (200°C/400°F, Gas Mark 6) for 10 to 12 minutes until well risen and lightly golden.

Remove the pastries to a wire tray and make a split along the crinkled side of each pastry. Leave to cool.

For the filling, soften the cheese in a bowl. Add the caster sugar to the whipped cream and blend with the cheese. Stir in the chopped fruits. Make a 'pocket' in each pastry where it is split, and fill with the cheese and fruit mixture. Dust with sifted icing (confectioners') sugar. Makes 16 small pastries.

Lemon and Lime Gâteau

Metric/Imperial	*American*
250 g/8 oz full fat soft cheese	1 cup cream cheese
1 × 350 g/12 oz can condensed milk	1 × 12 oz can condensed milk
120 ml/4 fl oz lemon juice	½ cup lemon juice
8 individual trifle sponge cakes	8 individual dessert sponge shells
125 g/4 oz shelled pistachio nuts	1 cup shelled pistachio nuts
150 ml/¼ pint double cream	⅔ cup heavy cream
1 lime	1 lime

Carefully line a deep 20 cm/8 inch round cake tin (pan) with foil, allowing at least 5 cm/2 inches to stand above the cake tin (pan) rim.

Lemon and Lime Gâteau

Place the cheese in a bowl and beat with a wooden spoon until smooth. Gradually beat in the condensed milk. Add the lemon juice and beat until thick. Leave to set in a cool place.

Split each sponge cake (shell) in half horizontally. Arrange a layer over the bottom of the tin (pan), cutting to fit. Spread $\frac{1}{3}$ of the filling over the sponge base and cover with another layer of sponge. Repeat with another $\frac{1}{3}$ of the filling and the remaining sponge slices. Fold over the foil and chill for at least 3 hours.

Place the pistachio nuts in a pan with boiling water to cover. Boil for 1 minute, then drain and slip off the skins. Chop the nuts. Fold back the foil from the cheesecake and invert to a serving plate. Peel off the foil. Cover with the remaining filling and coat the sides with chopped nuts. Whip the cream until stiff and pipe rosettes of cream around the edge of the cake and in the centre. Thinly slice the lime, then cut each slice into quarters. Place around the cake between the rosettes of cream. Serves 6-8.

Neapolitan Curd Tart, page 84

Neapolitan Curd Tart

Metric/Imperial	American
225 g/8 oz plain flour	2 cups all-purpose flour
pinch of salt	pinch of salt
75 g/3 oz caster sugar	6 tablespoons sugar
100 g/4 oz butter, softened	½ cup butter, softened
finely grated rind of ½ lemon	finely grated rind of ½ lemon
2 egg yolks	2 egg yolks
Filling:	*Filling:*
350 g/12 oz Ricotta or curd cheese	¾ lb Ricotta or curd cheese
75 g/3 oz caster sugar	6 tablespoons sugar
3 eggs, well beaten	3 eggs, well beaten
50 g/2 oz blanched almonds, finely chopped	½ cup finely chopped blanched almonds
75 g/3 oz candied peel, finely chopped	½ cup finely chopped candied peel
finely grated rind of ½ lemon	finely grated rind of ½ lemon
finely grated rind of ½ orange	finely grated rind of ½ orange
¼ teaspoon vanilla essence	¼ teaspoon vanilla extract
icing sugar for dusting	confectioners' sugar for dusting

Sift flour, salt and sugar together and make a well in the centre. Put the butter, lemon rind and egg yolks into the well. Mix all the ingredients to a firm, smooth dough and chill in the refrigerator.

To make the filling, rub the cheese through a sieve (strainer) into a basin and beat in the sugar. Gradually beat in the eggs, followed by all the remaining ingredients.

Roll out the pastry and line a 20 cm/8 inch flan ring. Fill the flan with the cheese mixture and smooth the surface. Roll out the pastry trimmings thinly, cut into 1 cm/½ inch wide strips with a fluted roller and use to make a criss-cross pattern over the top of the flan.

Bake for about 45 minutes in the centre of a preheated moderate oven (180°C/350°F, Gas Mark 4). Serve cold, dusted with icing (confectioners') sugar. Makes 6 slices.

Raspberry Cheese Charlotte

Metric/Imperial	American
16 sponge fingers	16 lady fingers
sherry	sherry
250 g/8 oz raspberries	¾ pint raspberries
juice of 1 orange	juice of 1 orange
75 g/3 oz caster sugar	6 tablespoons sugar
250 g/8 oz full fat soft cheese	1 cup cream cheese
3 eggs, separated	3 eggs, separated
2 tablespoons brandy	2 tablespoons brandy
2 tablespoons gelatine	2 tablespoons unflavored gelatin
5 tablespoons water	⅓ cup water
300 ml/½ pint double or whipping cream, lightly whipped	1¼ cups heavy or whipping cream, lightly whipped
To decorate:	*To decorate:*
150 ml/¼ pint double or whipping cream, whipped	⅔ cup heavy or whipping cream, whipped
raspberries	raspberries

Trim one end of each sponge finger (lady finger) so that it has a flat base. Moisten the sponge fingers with a little sherry. Use, sugar side in, to line the sides of a lightly buttered 18 to 20 cm/7 to 8 inch round spring-release tin (springform pan).

Put the raspberries into a blender with the orange juice and sugar and blend until smooth. Soften the cheese in a mixing bowl. Beat in the egg yolks, brandy and the raspberry purée. Put the gelatine and water into a small heatproof bowl over a saucepan of hot water and stir until the gelatine has dissolved. Stir the gelatine into the cheese and raspberry mixture. Leave on one side until the mixture is on the point of setting.

Whisk the egg whites until stiff. Fold the cream and the egg whites lightly but thoroughly into the cheese mixture. Spoon into the sponge-lined tin (pan). Chill for 3 to 4 hours or until the filling is set.

Carefully remove the charlotte from the tin (pan). Decorate with whipped cream and raspberries. Serves 6.

Edam Dip (Photograph: Dutch Dairy Bureau)

Edam Dip

Metric/Imperial	American
1 × 2 kg/4 lb whole Edam cheese	1 × 4 lb whole Edam cheese
150 ml/¼ pint plain yogurt	⅔ cup plain yogurt
250 g/8 oz cooked prawns, peeled	1⅓ cups cooked shrimp, shelled
2 sticks celery, chopped	2 stalks celery, chopped
salt	salt
freshly ground pepper	freshly ground pepper
600 ml/1 pint milk	2½ cups milk
To serve:	*To serve:*
sticks of celery, carrot and cucumber	stalks of celery
cauliflower sprigs	carrot and cucumber sticks
crackers	cauliflower sprigs
	crackers

Insert a sharp pointed knife into the top ⅓ of the Edam and make a deep zig-zag cut all the way round. Ease off the top. Scoop out the cheese from the base to leave a shell. Grate the cheese.

Mix the grated cheese with the yogurt, prawns (shrimp), celery and salt and pepper to taste. Gradually blend in the milk to a soft consistency. Spoon back into the Edam shell. Serve on a tray surrounded by the crudités and crackers. Serves 8-10.

Blue Cheese Dip

Metric/Imperial	American
125 g/4 oz Danish Blue cheese, crumbled	1 cup crumbled blue cheese
2 tablespoons mayonnaise	2 tablespoons mayonnaise
150 ml/¼ pint whipping cream, lightly whipped	⅔ cup whipping cream, lightly whipped
freshly ground pepper	freshly ground pepper
sliced cucumber, to garnish	sliced cucumber, for garnish

Using a fork or hand-held electric beater, mash the cheese. Beat in the mayonnaise until smooth. Lightly fold in the whipped cream and add pepper to taste.

Turn into a serving bowl and chill for about 1 hour. Garnish with cucumber twists. Serves 6-8.

Variation

Add ½ green or red pepper, cored, seeded and finely chopped.

Mustard Cheese Truffles

Metric/Imperial	American
250 g/8 oz full fat soft cheese	1 cup cream cheese
125 g/4 oz blue cheese, crumbled	1 cup crumbled blue cheese
2 teaspoons French mustard	2 teaspoons Dijon mustard
freshly ground pepper	freshly ground pepper
4-5 slices pumpernickel bread	4-5 slices pumpernickel bread

Beat the cheeses together in a bowl until smooth. Stir in the mustard and pepper to taste. Using a teaspoon, shape and roll the mixture into balls the size of walnuts.

Break the pumpernickel slices into small pieces and process briefly in a blender or foodprocessor, until fine breadcrumbs are produced. Coat the cheese balls in the crumbs and chill for at least 2 hours before serving. Makes about 24 truffles.

Cheese Squares

Metric/Imperial	American
75 g/3 oz plain flour	¾ cup all-purpose flour
75 g/3 oz margarine	6 tablespoons margarine
75 g/3 oz Cheddar cheese; grated	¾ cup grated Cheddar cheese
1 egg, beaten	1 egg, beaten
salt	salt
chopped walnuts or cayenne, to garnish	chopped walnuts or cayenne, to garnish

Sift the flour into a bowl. Rub (cut) in the fat until the mixture resembles fine crumbs. Stir in the cheese and knead to a soft dough. Wrap the dough in plastic wrap and chill for 30 minutes.

Roll out the dough thinly and cut into 3.5 cm/1½ inch squares, then cut the squares in half to form triangles. Mix the egg with a little salt and brush over the cheese triangles. Sprinkle with cayenne or walnuts. Bake in a preheated moderately hot oven (200°C/400°F, Gas Mark 6) for about 10 minutes, or until crisp and golden. Cool on a wire tray. Makes about 30.

Auvergne Triangles

Metric/Imperial	American
1 × 227 g/8 oz packet frozen puff pastry, thawed	1 × ½ lb package frozen puff pastry, thawed
250 g/8 oz Bleu d'Auvergne	½ lb Bleu d'Auvergne
1 beaten egg, to glaze	1 beaten egg, to glaze

Roll out the pastry thinly on a lightly floured board to a rectangle 40 × 20 cm/16 × 8 inches and cut the pastry into 10 cm/4 inch squares. Divide the cheese into 8 triangular portions. Place a piece of cheese on one half of each pastry square. Brush the edges with beaten egg. Fold the pastry over to form a triangle and pinch the edges together to seal.

Brush the cheese triangles with egg and make two slits in the top to allow the steam to escape. Place on a dampened baking sheet. Bake in a preheated hot oven (230°C/450°F, Gas Mark 8) for 10 to 15 minutes or until golden brown. Serve warm. Makes 8.

Cheese Pastry

Metric/Imperial	American
75 g/3 oz plain flour	¾ cup all-purpose flour
50 g/2 oz butter	¼ cup butter
75 g/3 oz mature Cheddar cheese, grated	¾ cup grated sharp Cheddar cheese
½ teaspoon salt	½ teaspoon salt
pinch of dry mustard	pinch of dry mustard
pinch of cayenne pepper	pinch of cayenne
1 egg yolk	1 egg yolk
½ teaspoon lemon juice	½ teaspoon lemon juice

Sift the flour into a mixing bowl. Rub (cut) in the butter until the mixture resembles coarse breadcrumbs. Mix in the cheese, salt, mustard and cayenne. Beat the egg yolk with the lemon juice, add to the flour mixture, and mix to form a dough. (If necessary, add a little iced water, but the dough should be soft, not sticky.) Wrap in plastic wrap and chill until required. Use in the following ways:

Cheese Biscuits (Crackers) Roll out the dough thinly and cut into small rounds with a floured cutter. Bake in a preheated moderately hot oven (200°C/400°F, Gas Mark 6) for 5 to 7 minutes, or until crisp. Makes about 36.

Cheese Straws Roll out the dough to a strip about 10 cm/4 inches wide and trim the edges. With a 6 cm/2½ inch cutter, cut three rounds from the dough and stamp out the middles, or cut with a sharp knife, to make hollow circles. Cut the remaining dough into straws and arrange all the dough shapes on a greased baking sheet. Bake in a preheated moderately hot oven (200°C/400°F, Gas Mark 6) for 5 to 7 minutes, or until crisp and golden. Cool on a wire tray, and arrange the straws in bundles pushed through the pastry circles. Makes about 30.

Helpful Hint
Hard cheeses store better than other kinds. If they do grow a surface mould it can easily be scraped off.

Christmas Cheese

Metric/Imperial	American
250 g/8 oz Blue Stilton cheese, grated	2 cups grated Blue Stilton cheese
250 g/8 oz Wensleydale or Lancashire cheese, grated	2 cups grated Wensleydale or Lancashire cheese
2 tablespoons port	2 tablespoons port
75 g/3 oz walnuts, chopped	¾ cup chopped walnuts
To serve:	To serve:
crackers	crackers
celery sticks, spring onions	celery stalks, scallions

Put the cheeses in a bowl and stir in the port. Beat the mixture with a hand-held electric beater or wooden spoon until smooth. Turn out on to a piece of plastic wrap or waxed paper, form into a ball and wrap well. Chill for at least 12 hours. Just before serving roll in the chopped nuts. Serve with crackers, celery sticks (stalks) and spring onions (scallions). Serves 8-10.

Christmas Cheese (Photograph: National Dairy Council)

Cocktail Cheesecake

These cocktail cheesecakes should be served like canapés, as an accompaniment to drinks.

Metric/Imperial
450 g/1 lb full fat soft cream
cheese
4 eggs, separated
200 ml/⅓ pint double or
whipping cream
175 g/6 oz cooked ham,
finely chopped or
minced
salt
freshly ground pepper
40 g/1½ oz powdered
gelatine dissolved in
120 ml/4 fl oz water
toasted fine breadcrumbs
or chopped fresh parsley
or finely chopped toasted
nuts

American
2 cups cream cheese
4 eggs, separated
⅞ cup heavy or whipping
cream
¾ cup finely chopped or
ground cooked ham
salt
freshly ground pepper
3 envelopes unflavored
gelatin dissolved in ½
cup water
toasted fine bread crumbs
or chopped fresh parsley
or finely chopped toasted
nuts

For moulding these cocktail cheesecakes, you can use any smooth, straight-sided, narrow metal moulds or squat glasses. The quantities given in this recipe are sufficient for about 5 good-size glasses.

Grease the moulds. Soften the cheese in a large mixing bowl. Beat in the egg yolks, cream, ham (or other chosen ingredient) and salt and pepper to taste. Beat the dissolved gelatine into the cheese mixture. Leave on one side until the mixture is on the point of setting.

Whisk the egg whites until stiff and fold lightly but thoroughly into the cheese mixture. Spoon the mixture into the prepared moulds and shake each gently to level the surface. Chill for 3 to 4 hours or until set.

Wrap a cloth wrung out in hot water around each mould to loosen the cheesecakes. Carefully unmould on to a greased surface. Roll in toasted breadcrumbs, chopped parsley or toasted nuts to give an even coating. Chill for a further 30 minutes. Cut into thin slices. Serves 24-30.

Camembert Beignets

Metric/Imperial	American
50 g/2 oz butter	¼ cup butter
40 g/1½ oz plain flour	6 tablespoons all-purpose
250 ml/8 fl oz water	flour
3 eggs, separated	1 cup water
250 g/8 oz Camembert	3 eggs, separated
cheese	½ lb Camembert cheese
salt	salt
oil for deep frying	oil for deep frying
sauce tartare, to serve	sauce tartare, to serve

Melt the butter in a saucepan, remove from the heat and add the flour all at once. Return to the heat and add the water, stirring continuously. Bring to the boil and continue stirring until the mixture thickens. Remove from the heat and gradually beat in the eggs until the mixture becomes smooth and glossy.

Remove the crust and then cut the cheese into small pieces. Beat the cheese into the hot sauce and add salt to taste. Cool slightly. Whisk the egg whites until stiff and fold into the cheese mixture.

Heat the oil in a deep-fat frier to 180°C/350°F or until a stale (dry) bread cube turns golden in 60 seconds. Deep fry tablespoons of the mixture in batches until golden brown and crisp, turning them over during frying. Drain on kitchen paper towels and keep hot. Makes about 24.

FONDUES

A fondue party is a marvellously simple way of entertaining friends informally. Fondues take very little time to prepare, are fun to eat and easy to serve – everyone helps them-selves.

Traditionally the national dish of Switzerland, cheese fondue consists of cheese melted in wine. The name comes from the French verb 'fondre', which means 'to melt or dissolve'.

Cheese fondues originally came into existence because the winter snows cut the villagers off from the main towns. The villagers had to rely on locally produced foods – bread, wine and cheese. As the winter months wore on the cheese became drier and more unpalatable, but when melted in wine it became a delightful and tasty dish – one that is now highly regarded by gourmets and cheese-lovers all over the world.

The type of cheese used for a fondue is important – use good quality mature (sharp) cheese. Emmental and Gruyère (Swiss cheese) give the right texture and for the best results use at least a proportion of these for good flavour and smoothness.

The best wine for fondue is a dry white (Chablis, Hock or Riesling) and it is best to warm it slightly before adding the cheese. If the completed fondue is too thin, add more grated cheese or cornflour (cornstarch) blended with a little wine; if it is too thick, add a little more warmed wine. Guests should be provided with long-handled forks for spearing cubes of crusty bread. The choice of bread is important too, it must be crisp and have plenty of crust. Allow 250 g/8 oz (½ lb) bread per person and offer it around so each person has some on his plate. To keep the cube of bread firmly attached, push the fork prongs through the soft part of the bread first, then through the crust. Everyone dips their own bread into the fondue, stirring in a figure of eight until coated in cheese.

When only a little of the fondue is left in the bottom of the dish, it forms a crust, known as the 'crouton'. The host should now pour over a little Kirsch and set it alight. Once the flames die down, everyone can share this delicacy.

It is usual to serve the same white wine as that used in the fondue, although traditionally the only drink that is served is a glass of Kirsch halfway through the meal. This is known as the *'coup de milieu'* which is said to promote digestion and stimulate the appetite.

Equipment

The Swiss Fondue dish is called a *'caquelon'* and is ideally made of earthenware or enamelled cast iron. This heavy thick pot is wide and shallow to ensure that the heat is evenly distributed.

A methylated or butane burner, which is safe for use on the table, is essential. A heatproof mat or tray beneath it will give added protection.

Swiss Cheese Fondue

Swiss Cheese Fondue

Metric/Imperial	*American*
2 garlic cloves, halved	2 garlic cloves, halved
450 ml/¾ pint dry white wine	2 cups dry white wine
250 g/8 oz Gruyère cheese, grated	2 cups grated Swiss cheese
250 g/8 oz Emmental cheese, grated	2 cups grated Emmental cheese
2 tablespoons cornflour	2 tablespoons cornstarch
small glass of Kirsch	small glass of Kirsch
freshly ground black pepper	freshly ground black pepper
crusty bread, to serve	crusty bread, to serve

Rub the cut sides of the garlic around the sides and bottom of the fondue pot. Pour in the white wine and heat gently. Stir in the cheese and cook over a very low heat, stirring until the cheese melts.

Blend the cornflour (cornstarch) with the Kirsch and add to the melted cheese mixture with pepper to taste, stirring constantly without boiling. Serve with cubes of bread speared on fondue forks and stir each into the fondue until well coated with cheese. Serves 6-8.

The publishers would like to thank the following photographers:
Bryce Attwell 34-5, 38, 39, 46, 55; Robert Estall 7, 19, 31; Robert Golden 11, 43, 59, 63, 82, 83; Melvin Grey 78, 79; Paul Kemp 2-3, 14, 94; Norman Nicholls 70; Charlie Stebbings 74; Paul Williams 67. Calorie chart page 11: Slimming Magazine's *Your Greatest Guide to Calories*.
Illustrator: Oriel Bath.